WHAT'S COOKING
low fat

Kathryn Hawkins

This edition published
in 1999 by
Parragon
Queen Street House
4 Queen Street
Bath BA1 1HE

ISBN: 0-75252-935-8 (Paperback)
ISBN:0-75253-225-1 (Hardback)

Printed in Singapore

Produced by Haldane Mason, London

Acknowledgements
Art Director: Ron Samuels
Editorial Director: Sydney Francis
Editorial Consultant: Christopher Fagg
Managing Editor: Jo-Anne Cox
Editor: Lydia Darbyshire
Design: Digital Artworks Partnership Ltd
Photography: Iain Bagwell
Home Economist: Kathryn Hawkins
Nutritional information: Anne Sheasby and Annette Yates

Note
Cup measurements in this book are for American cups.
Tablespoons are assumed to be 15 ml. Unless otherwise stated,
milk is assumed to be full fat, eggs are medium and pepper is freshly
ground black pepper. The calorie counts and fat content
analysis do not include the serving suggestions.

Contents

Introduction

No one who has more than a passing interest in their health can be unaware of the problems associated with a diet that contains too much fat. A high level of fat consumption is implicated in obesity – and all that that entails – coronary disease, diabetes and even cancer. The message that we should all cut down on the fat in our diets is reinforced every time we go shopping, and it is almost impossible to walk around a supermarket without being beset on all sides by labels proclaiming low-fat this, reduced-fat that and no-fat the other.

Cutting the amount of fat in our diets is, of course, an effective way to lose weight, simply because it will reduce the number of calories we consume, as well as reducing the likelihood that we will contract a serious disease. However, before we cut fat out of our lives completely, it is important to remember that we all need to include a certain amount of fat in our daily intake of food if our bodies are to function properly. Essential fatty acids are needed to build cell membranes and for other vital bodily functions. Our brain tissue, nerve sheaths and bone marrow need fat, for example, and we all need fat to protect vital organs such as our liver, kidneys and heart.

Nutritionists suggest that we should aim to cut our intake of fat to 27-30 per cent of our total daily calorie intake. If your average diet totals 2000 calories, this will mean eating no more than about 75 g/2¾ oz of fat a day. As a guide, bear in mind that most people consume about 40 per cent of their daily calories in the form of fat. Remember, however, that if you are being treated for any medical condition, you must discuss with your family doctor or practice nurse the changes you propose making in your diet before you begin your new regime.

When you are thinking about reducing your intake of fat, it is important to know that fats can be broadly divided into saturated and unsaturated fat. Saturated fats are those that are solid at room temperature, and they are found mainly in animal products – butter and cheese, high-fat meats (sausages, pâté, streaky bacon), cakes, chocolate, potato crisps, biscuits, coconut and hydrogenated (hardened) vegetable or fish oils. Unsaturated fats are healthier – but they are still fats. Your target should be a reduction to 8 per cent of your daily calories in the form of saturated facts, with the remainder in the form of unsaturated fats. These are usually liquid at room temperature and come from vegetable sources – olive oil, ground nut oil, sunflower oil, safflower oil and corn oil. Remember, though, that oil is only another name for liquid fat. Using oil instead of margarine or butter to fry onions or garlic will do nothing to reduce your overall intake of fat.

INGREDIENTS

One of the simplest and most beneficial changes you can make in your diet is to change from full-fat milk, cream, cheese and yogurt to a low- or reduced-fat equivalent. Semi-skimmed milk, for example, has all the nutritional benefits of whole milk but 10 g/⅓ oz of fat per pint compared with 23 g/¾ oz of fat per pint in whole milk. Use skimmed milk to make custards and sauces and you will not notice the difference in flavour. Low-fat yogurt or fromage frais mixed with chopped chives is a delicious and healthy alternative to butter or sour cream.

Most vegetables are naturally low in fat and can be used to make a meal of meat or fish go further. Recent nutritional research indicates that we should all aim to eat five portions of fresh fruit and vegetables every day because they contain what are known as antioxidant vitamins, including beta carotene (which creates vitamin A in the body) and vitamins C and E. The antioxidant vitamins in vegetables are thought to help prevent a number of degenerative illnesses (including cancer, heart diseases, arthritis and even ageing of the skin) and to protect the body from the harmful effects of pollution and ultraviolet light, which can damage the body's cells. Phytochemicals, which occur naturally in plants, are thought to be instrumental in the fight against cancer.

Steaming is the best way to cook vegetables to preserve their goodness. Boiling can, for example, destroy up to three-quarters of the vitamin C present in green vegetables. If you have to boil, cook the vegetables as quickly as possible and avoid over-cooking, which also destroys the carotene.

If you have time, it is a good idea to make your own stock to use as the basis of casseroles and soups. The ready-made stocks and stock cubes that are available from shops are often high in salt and artificial flavourings. Instead, use fresh herbs and spices in the water in which vegetables have been cooked or in which dried mushrooms have been soaked. Liquids in which meat and fish of various kinds have been cooked should be saved, too. Chill the liquid in the refrigerator and you will easily be able to remove and discard the fat, which will have risen to the top of the container and solidified.

Pastas, noodles, pulses and grains can all be used in the low-fat diet, and they are useful for bulking out dishes. Pasta is available in a wide range of shapes and patterns, and it is an excellent food for boosting your carbohydrate intake. Inadequate intake of carbohydrate can result in fatigue and poor energy

levels. Wholemeal (whole wheat) pasta is also particularly high in fibre, which helps to speed the passage of waste material through the digestive system. Stir cooked brown rice into soups and casseroles to thicken them, or mix one part red lentils with three parts lean minced (ground) beef to make a smaller amount of meat go further. Before you buy, check that noodles and pastas have not been enriched with egg. Look out instead for wholemeal (whole wheat) or rice varieties.

EQUIPMENT

Money spent on good quality non-stick pans and cookware will not be wasted. Not only will they directly reduce the amount of fat needed for cooking, but they will save you time because they are easier to clean. Remember to use plastic implements or wooden spoons with non-stick pans so that you do not scratch the surface.

A ridged frying pan makes it possible to cook with the minimum amount of fat or oil, because the fat drips down between the ridges rather than being absorbed by the food. Woks are useful – though not essential – for stir fries. When you are stir frying, use the smallest possible amount of oil. Keep the heat constant and the food moving to ensure quick, even cooking. Use a non-stick wok, which will help you cut down still further on the amount of oil you need.

Use a perforated or slotted spoon to remove food from the frying pan, so that cooking juices are left behind. Absorbent kitchen paper is useful both for draining surface oil and fat from food that has just been cooked, but it can also be used to mop up food that rises to the top of a saucepan during cooking. Use plain, unpatterned paper so that no dye is transferred to the food.

Soups & Starters

Many favourite snacks and starters – especially those that we buy ready-prepared on supermarket shelves and in cans – are surprisingly high in fat. Next time, before you buy, think instead about making some of the appetizing recipes on the following pages – they will get your meal off to a wonderful low-fat start.

Soups are a traditional first course, but, served with crusty bread, they can also be a satisfying meal in their own right. Although it does take a little longer, consider making your own stock by using the liquor left after cooking vegetables and the juices from fish and meat that have been used as the base of casseroles. Use a potato to thicken your soups rather than stirring in the traditional thickener of flour and water – or, worse, flour and fat.

If you want a change from soup, try a few starters such as a light Cheesy Ham and Celery Savoury or Parsleyed Chicken and Ham Pâté served with a refreshing salad and crisp breads or flavour-filled Spinach Cheese Moulds.

Chicken & Asparagus Soup

This light, clear soup has a delicate flavour of asparagus and herbs. Use a good quality stock for best results.

Serves 4

CALORIES PER SERVING: 236 • FAT CONTENT PER SERVING: 2.9 G

INGREDIENTS

225 g/8 oz fresh asparagus
850 ml/1^{1}/$_2$ pints/3^{3}/$_4$ cups fresh
   chicken stock
150 ml/5 fl oz/^{2}/$_3$ cup dry white wine

1 sprig each fresh parsley, dill
   and tarragon
1 garlic clove
60 g/2 oz/^{1}/$_3$ cup vermicelli
   rice noodles

350 g/12 oz lean cooked chicken,
   finely shredded
salt and white pepper
1 small leek, shredded, to garnish

1 Wash the asparagus and trim away the woody ends. Cut each spear into pieces 4 cm/ 1½ inches long.

2 Pour the stock and wine into a large saucepan and bring to the boil.

3 Wash the herbs and tie them with clean string. Peel the garlic clove and add, with the herbs, to the saucepan together with the asparagus and noodles. Cover and simmer for 5 minutes.

4 Stir in the chicken and plenty of seasoning. Simmer gently for a further 3-4 minutes until heated through.

5 Trim the leek, slice it down the centre and wash under running water to remove any dirt. Shake dry and shred finely.

6 Remove the herbs and garlic from the pan and discard. Ladle the soup into warm bowls, sprinkle with shredded leek and serve at once.

VARIATION

You can use any of your favourite herbs in this recipe, but choose those with a subtle flavour so that they do not overpower the asparagus. Small, tender asparagus spears give the best results and flavour.

COOK'S TIP

Rice noodles contain no fat and are an ideal substitute for egg noodles.

Beef, Water Chestnut & Rice Soup

*Strips of tender lean beef are combined with crisp water chestnuts
and cooked rice in a tasty beef broth with a tang of orange.*

Serves 4

CALORIES PER SERVING: 205 • FAT CONTENT PER SERVING: 4.5 G

INGREDIENTS

350 g/12 oz lean beef (such as rump
   or sirloin)
1 litre/1³/₄ pints/1 quart fresh
   beef stock
cinnamon stick, broken
2 star anise
2 tbsp dark soy sauce

2 tbsp dry sherry
3 tbsp tomato purée (paste)
115 g/4 oz can water chestnuts,
   drained and sliced
175 g/6 oz/3 cups cooked white rice
1 tsp zested orange rind
6 tbsp orange juice

salt and pepper

TO GARNISH:
strips of orange rind
2 tbsp chives, snipped

1 Carefully trim away any fat
from the beef. Cut the beef
into thin strips and then place into
a large saucepan.

2 Pour over the stock and add
the cinnamon, star anise, soy
sauce, sherry, tomato purée (paste)
and water chestnuts. Bring to the
boil, skimming away any surface
scum with a flat ladle. Cover the
pan and simmer gently for about
20 minutes or until the beef
is tender.

3 Skim the soup with a flat ladle
to remove any scum again.
Remove and discard the cinnamon
and star anise and blot the surface
with absorbent kitchen paper to
remove any fat.

4 Stir in the rice, orange rind
and juice. Adjust the
seasoning if necessary. Heat
through for 2–3 minutes before
ladling into warm bowls. Serve
garnished with strips of orange
rind and snipped chives.

VARIATION

*Omit the rice for a
lighter soup that is
an ideal starter for an
Oriental meal of many
courses. For a more substantial soup
that would be a meal in its own
right, add diced vegetables such as
carrot, (bell) pepper, sweetcorn or
courgette (zucchini).*

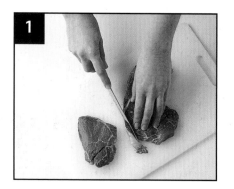

Winter Beef & Vegetable Soup

This comforting broth is perfect for a cold day and is sure to warm you up.

Serves 4

CALORIES PER SERVING: 161 • FAT CONTENT PER SERVING: 3.3 G

INGREDIENTS

60 g/2 oz/¹⁄₃ cup pearl barley
1.2 litres/2 pints/5 cups fresh beef
   stock
1 tsp dried mixed herbs
225 g/8 oz lean rump or sirloin beef

1 large carrot, diced
1 leek, shredded
1 medium onion, chopped
2 sticks celery, sliced
salt and pepper

2 tbsp fresh parsley, chopped,
   to garnish
crusty bread, to serve

1 Place the pearl barley in a large saucepan. Pour over the stock and add the mixed herbs. Bring to the boil, cover and simmer for 10 minutes.

2 Meanwhile, trim any fat from the beef and cut the meat into thin strips.

3 Skim away any scum that has risen to the top of the stock with a flat ladle.

4 Add the beef, carrot, leek, onion and celery to the pan.

Bring back to the boil, cover and simmer for about 20 minutes or until the meat and vegetables are just tender.

5 Skim away any remaining scum that has risen to the top of the soup with a flat ladle. Blot the surface with absorbent kitchen paper to remove any fat. Adjust the seasoning according to taste.

6 Ladle the soup into warm bowls and sprinkle with freshly chopped parsley. Serve accompanied with crusty bread.

VARIATION

This soup is just as delicious made with lean lamb or pork fillet. A vegetarian version can be made by omitting the beef and beef stock and using vegetable stock instead. Just before serving, stir in 175 g/ 6 oz fresh bean curd (tofu), drained and diced. An even more substantial soup can be made by adding other root vegetables, such as swede or turnip, instead of, or as well as, the carrot.

Mediterranean-style Fish Soup

Juicy chunks of fish and sumptuous shellfish are cooked in a flavoursome tomato, herb and wine stock. Serve with toasted bread rubbed with garlic.

Serves 4

CALORIES PER SERVING: 270 • FAT CONTENT PER SERVING: 5.3 G

INGREDIENTS

1 tbsp olive oil
1 large onion, chopped
2 garlic cloves, finely chopped
425 ml/15 fl oz/1¾ cups fresh
   fish stock
150 ml/5 fl oz/⅔ cup dry white wine
1 bay leaf
1 sprig each fresh thyme, rosemary
   and oregano

450 g/1 lb firm white fish fillets (such
   as cod, monkfish or halibut),
   skinned and cut into 2.5 cm/1 inch
   cubes
450 g/1 lb fresh mussels, prepared
400 g/14 oz can chopped tomatoes
225 g/8 oz peeled prawns (shrimp),
   thawed if frozen

salt and pepper
sprigs of thyme, to garnish

TO SERVE:
lemon wedges
4 slices toasted French bread, rubbed
   with cut garlic clove

1 Heat the oil in a large saucepan and gently fry the onion and garlic for 2–3 minutes until just softened.

2 Pour in the stock and wine and bring to the boil. Tie the bay leaf and herbs together with clean string and add to the saucepan together with the fish and mussels. Stir well, cover and simmer for 5 minutes.

3 Stir in the tomatoes and prawns (shrimp) and continue to cook for a further 3–4 minutes until piping hot and the fish is cooked through.

4 Discard the herbs and any mussels that have not opened. Season to taste, then ladle into warm bowls. Garnish with sprigs of fresh thyme and serve with lemon wedges and toasted bread.

COOK'S TIP

Traditionally, the toasted bread is placed at the bottom of the bowl and the soup spooned over the top. For convenience, look out for prepared, cooked shellfish mixes, which you could use instead of fresh fish. Simply add to the soup with the tomatoes in step 3.

Tuscan Bean & Vegetable Soup

This thick, satisfying blend of beans and diced vegetables in a rich red wine and tomato stock, based on an Italian favourite, makes an ideal simple supper.

Serves 4

CALORIES PER SERVING: 156 • FAT CONTENT PER SERVING: 1.5 G

INGREDIENTS

1 medium onion, chopped
1 garlic clove, finely chopped
2 celery sticks, sliced
1 large carrot, diced
400 g/14 oz can chopped tomatoes
150 ml/5 fl oz/^{2}/$_3$ cup Italian dry
   red wine

1.2 litres/2 pints/5 cups fresh
   vegetable stock
1 tsp dried oregano
425 g/15 oz can mixed beans
   and pulses
2 medium courgettes
   (zucchini), diced

1 tbsp tomato purée (paste)
salt and pepper

TO SERVE:
low-fat pesto sauce (see page 146)
crusty bread

1 Place the prepared onion, garlic, celery and carrot in a large saucepan. Stir in the tomatoes, red wine, vegetable stock and oregano.

2 Bring the vegetable mixture to the boil, cover and leave to simmer for 15 minutes. Stir the beans and courgettes (zucchini) into the mixture, and continue to cook, uncovered, for a further 5 minutes.

3 Add the tomato purée (paste) to the mixture and season well with salt and pepper to taste. Then heat through, stirring occasionally, for a further 2–3 minutes, but do not allow the mixture to boil again.

4 Ladle the soup into warm bowls and serve with a spoonful of low-fat pesto (see page 146) on each portion and accompanied with crusty bread.

VARIATION

For a more substantial soup, add 350 g/12 oz diced lean cooked chicken or turkey with the tomato purée (paste) in step 3.

Lentil, Pasta & Vegetable Soup

*Packed with the flavour of garlic, this soup is a filling supper
dish when it is served with crusty bread and a crisp salad.*

Serves 4

CALORIES PER SERVING: 378 • FAT CONTENT PER SERVING: 4.9 G

INGREDIENTS

1 tbsp olive oil
1 medium onion, chopped
4 garlic cloves, finely chopped
350 g/12 oz carrot, sliced
1 stick celery, sliced
225 g/8 oz/1¼ cups red lentils

600 ml/1 pint/2½ cups fresh
  vegetable stock
700 ml/1¼ pint/scant 3 cups
  boiling water
150 g/5½ oz/scant 1 cup pasta
150 ml/5 fl oz/⅔ cup natural low-fat

fromage frais (unsweetened
  yogurt), plus extra to serve
salt and pepper
2 tbsp fresh parsley, chopped,
  to garnish

1 Heat the oil in a large saucepan and gently fry the prepared onion, garlic, carrot and celery, stirring gently, for 5 minutes until the vegetables begin to soften.

2 Add the lentils, stock and boiling water. Season well, stir and bring back to the boil. Simmer, uncovered, for 15 minutes until the lentils are completely tender. Allow to cool for 10 minutes.

3 Meanwhile, bring another saucepan of water to the boil and cook the pasta according to the instructions on the packet. Drain well and set aside.

4 Place the soup in a blender and process until smooth. Return to a saucepan and add the pasta. Bring back to a simmer and heat for 2–3 minutes until piping hot. Remove from the heat and stir in the fromage frais (yogurt). Adjust the seasoning if necessary.

5 Serve sprinkled with freshly ground black pepper and chopped parsley and with extra fromage frais (yogurt) if wished.

COOK'S TIP

Avoid boiling the soup once the fromage frais (yogurt) has been added. Otherwise it will separate and become watery, spoiling the appearance of the soup.

Creamy Sweetcorn Soup

Based on a traditional chowder recipe, this filling combination of tender sweetcorn kernels and a creamy stock is extra delicious with lean diced ham sprinkled on top.

Serves 4

CALORIES PER SERVING: 346 • FAT CONTENT PER SERVING: 2.4 G

INGREDIENTS

1 large onion, chopped
1 large potato, peeled and diced
1 litre/1³/4 pints/1 quart
   skimmed milk
1 bay leaf
¹/2 tsp ground nutmeg

450 g/1 lb sweetcorn kernels, canned
   or frozen, drained or thawed
1 tbsp cornflour (cornstarch)
3 tbsp cold water
4 tbsp natural low-fat fromage frais
   (unsweetened yogurt)

salt and pepper

TO GARNISH:
100 g/3¹/2 oz lean ham, diced
2 tbsp fresh chives, snipped

1 Place the onion and potato in a large saucepan and pour over the milk. Add the bay leaf, nutmeg and half the sweetcorn. Bring to the boil, cover and simmer gently for 15 minutes until the potato is softened. Stir the soup occasionally and keep the heat low so that the milk does not burn on the bottom of the pan.

2 Discard the bay leaf and leave the liquid to cool for 10 minutes. Transfer to a blender and

process for a few seconds. Alternatively, rub through a sieve.

3 Pour the smooth liquid into a saucepan. Blend the cornflour (cornstarch) with the cold water to make a paste and stir it into the soup.

4 Bring the soup back to the boil, stirring until it thickens, and add the remaining sweetcorn. Heat through for 2–3 minutes until piping hot.

5 Remove from the heat and season well. Stir in the fromage frais (yogurt). Ladle the soup into warm bowls and serve sprinkled with the diced ham and snipped chives.

VARIATION

For a more substantial soup, add 225 g/8 oz flaked white crab meat or peeled prawns (shrimp) in step 4.

Tomato & Red (Bell) Pepper Soup

*Sweet red (bell) peppers and tangy tomatoes are blended together
in a smooth vegetable soup that makes a perfect starter or light lunch.*

Serves 4

CALORIES PER SERVING: 93 • FAT CONTENT PER SERVING: 1 G

INGREDIENTS

2 large red (bell) peppers
1 large onion, chopped
2 sticks celery, trimmed and chopped
1 garlic clove, crushed

600 ml/1 pint/2¹/₂ cups fresh
 vegetable stock
2 bay leaves
2 x 400 g/14 oz cans plum tomatoes

salt and pepper
2 spring onions (scallions), finely
 shredded, to garnish
crusty bread, to serve

1 Preheat the grill (broiler) to hot. Halve and deseed the (bell) peppers, arrange them on the grill (broiler) rack and cook, turning occasionally, for 8–10 minutes until softened and charred.

2 Leave to cool slightly, then carefully peel off the charred skin. Reserving a small piece for garnish, chop the (bell) pepper flesh and place in a large saucepan.

3 Mix in the onion, celery and garlic. Add the stock and the bay leaves. Bring to the boil, cover and simmer for 15 minutes. Remove from the heat.

4 Stir in the tomatoes and transfer to a blender. Process for a few seconds until smooth. Return to the saucepan.

5 Season to taste and heat for 3–4 minutes until piping hot. Ladle into warm bowls and garnish with the reserved (bell) pepper cut into strips and the spring onion (scallion) floating on the top. Serve with crusty bread.

COOK'S TIP

If you prefer a coarser, more robust soup, lightly mash the tomatoes with a wooden spoon and omit the blending process in step 4.

Carrot, Apple & Celery Soup

*This fresh-tasting soup is ideal as a light starter. Use your favourite eating
(dessert) apple rather than a cooking variety, which will give too tart a flavour.*

Serves 4

CALORIES PER SERVING: 150 • FAT CONTENT PER SERVING: 1.4 G

INGREDIENTS

900 g/2 lb carrots, finely diced
1 medium onion, chopped
3 sticks celery, trimmed and diced
1 litre/1³/₄ pints/1 quart fresh
   vegetable stock

3 medium-sized eating
   (dessert) apples
2 tbsp tomato purée (paste)
1 bay leaf
2 tsp caster (superfine) sugar

¹/₄ large lemon
salt and pepper
celery leaves, washed and shredded,
   to garnish

1 Place the prepared carrots, onion and celery in a large saucepan and add the stock. Bring to the boil, cover and simmer for 10 minutes.

2 Meanwhile, peel, core and dice 2 of the apples. Add the pieces of apple, tomato purée (paste), bay leaf and caster (superfine) sugar to the saucepan and bring to the boil. Reduce the heat, half cover and allow to simmer for 20 minutes. Remove and discard the bay leaf.

3 Meanwhile, wash, core and cut the remaining apple into thin slices, leaving on the skin. Place the apple slices in a small saucepan and squeeze over the lemon juice. Heat gently and simmer for 1–2 minutes until tender. Drain and set aside.

4 Place the carrot and apple mixture in a blender or food processor and blend until smooth. Alternatively, press the mixture through a sieve with the back of a wooden spoon.

5 Gently re-heat the soup if necessary and season with salt and pepper to taste. Ladle the soup into warm bowls and serve topped with the reserved apple slices and shredded celery leaves.

COOK'S TIP

*Soaking light coloured fruit in
lemon juice helps to prevent it
from turning brown.*

Chilled Piquant Prawn (Shrimp) & Cucumber Soup

Serve this soup over ice on a warm summer day as a refreshing starter.
It has the fresh tang of yogurt and a dash of spice from the Tabasco sauce.

Serves 4

CALORIES PER SERVING: 104 • FAT CONTENT PER SERVING: 1 G

INGREDIENTS

1 cucumber, peeled and diced
400 ml/14 fl oz/1²/₃ cups fresh fish
   stock, chilled
150 ml/5 fl oz/²/₃ cup tomato juice
150 ml/5 fl oz/²/₃ cup low-fat
   natural (unsweetened) yogurt
150 ml/5 fl oz/²/₃ cup low-fat

fromage frais (or double the
   quantity of yogurt)
125 g/4¹/₂ oz peeled prawns
   (shrimp), thawed if frozen,
   roughly chopped
few drops Tabasco sauce
1 tbsp fresh mint, chopped

salt and white pepper
ice cubes, to serve

TO GARNISH:
sprigs of mint
cucumber slices
whole peeled prawns (shrimp)

1 Place the diced cucumber in a blender or food processor and work for a few seconds until smooth. Alternatively, chop the cucumber finely and push through a sieve.

2 Transfer the cucumber to a bowl. Stir in the stock, tomato juice, yogurt, fromage frais (if using) and prawns (shrimp), and mix well. Add the Tabasco sauce and season to taste.

3 Stir in the chopped mint, cover and chill for at least 2 hours.

4 Ladle the soup into glass bowls and add a few ice cubes. Serve garnished with mint, cucumber slices and whole prawns (shrimp).

VARIATION

Instead of prawns (shrimp), add white crab meat or minced chicken. For a vegetarian version of this soup, omit the prawns (shrimp) and add an extra 125 g/4¹/₂ oz finely diced cucumber. Use fresh vegetable stock instead of fish stock.

Rosy Melon & Strawberries

The combination of sweet melon and strawberries macerated in rosé wine and a hint of rose-water is a delightful start to a special meal.

Serves 4

CALORIES PER SERVING: 83 • FAT CONTENT PER SERVING: 0.2 G

INGREDIENTS

¹/₄ honeydew melon
¹/₂ Charentais or Cantaloupe melon
150 ml/5 fl oz/²/₃ cup rosé wine

2–3 tsp rose-water
175 g/6 oz small strawberries, washed and hulled

rose petals, to garnish

1 Scoop out the seeds from both melons with a spoon. Then carefully remove the skin, taking care not to remove too much flesh.

2 Cut the melon flesh into thin strips and place in a bowl. Pour over the wine and sufficient rose-water to taste. Mix together gently, cover and leave to chill in the refrigerator for at least 2 hours.

3 Halve the strawberries and carefully mix into the melon. Allow the melon and strawberries to stand at room temperature for about 15 minutes for the flavours to develop – if the melon is too cold, there will be little flavour.

4 Arrange on individual serving plates and serve sprinkled with a few rose petals.

COOK'S TIP

Rose-water is generally available from large pharmacies and leading supermarkets as well as from more specialist food suppliers.

COOK'S TIP

It does not matter whether the rosé wine is sweet or dry – although sweet wine contains more calories. Experiment with different types of melon. Varieties such as 'Sweet Dream' have whitish-green flesh, while Charentais melons, which have orange flesh, are fragrant and go better with a dry wine. If you wish, soak the strawberries in the wine with the melon, but always allow the fruit to return to room temperature before serving.

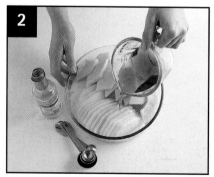

Italian Platter

*This popular hors d'oeuvre usually consists of vegetables soaked in olive oil
and accompanied with rich, creamy cheeses. Try this equally good low-fat version.*

Serves 4

CALORIES PER SERVING: 175 • FAT CONTENT PER SERVING: 7.6 G

INGREDIENTS

125 g/4¹/₂ oz reduced-fat Mozzarella
  cheese, drained
60 g/2 oz lean Parma ham
  (prosciutto)
400 g/14 oz can artichoke
  hearts, drained
4 ripe figs

1 small mango
few plain Grissini (bread sticks),
  to serve

FOR THE DRESSING:
1 small orange

1 tbsp passata (sieved tomatoes)
1 tsp wholegrain mustard
4 tbsp low-fat natural (unsweetened)
  yogurt
fresh basil leaves
salt and pepper

1 Cut the cheese into 12 sticks, 6.5 cm/2½ inches long. Remove the fat from the ham and slice the meat into 12 strips.

2 Carefully wrap a strip of ham around each stick of cheese and arrange them neatly on a serving platter.

3 Halve the artichoke hearts and cut the figs into quarters. Arrange them on the serving platter in groups.

4 Peel the mango, then slice it down each side of the large, flat central stone. Slice the flesh into strips and arrange them so that they form a fan shape on the serving platter.

5 To make the dressing, pare the rind from half the orange using a vegetable peeler. Cut the rind into small strips and place them in a bowl. Extract the juice from the orange and add it to the bowl containing the rind.

6 Add the passata (sieved tomatoes), mustard, yogurt and seasoning to the bowl and mix together. Shred the basil leaves and mix them into the dressing.

7 Spoon the dressing into a small dish and serve with the Italian Platter, accompanied with bread sticks.

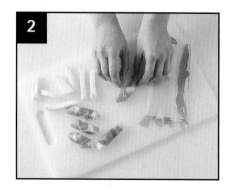

Breakfast Muffins

Try this filling breakfast or brunch idea for a good start to the day – a toasted muffin, topped with lean bacon, grilled tomato, mushrooms and a poached egg.

Serves 4

Calories per serving: 270 • Fat content per serving: 12.3 g

INGREDIENTS

2 wholemeal muffins
8 rashers lean back bacon, rinds
   removed

4 medium eggs
2 large tomatoes
2 large flat mushrooms

4 tbsp fresh vegetable stock
salt and pepper
1 small bunch fresh chives, snipped,
   to garnish

1 Preheat the grill (broiler) to medium. Cut the muffins in half and lightly toast them for 1–2 minutes on the open side. Set aside and keep warm.

2 Trim off all visible fat from the bacon and grill for 2–3 minutes on each side until cooked through. Drain on absorbent kitchen paper and keep warm.

3 Place 4 egg-poaching rings in a frying pan (skillet) and pour in enough water to cover the base of the pan. Bring to the boil and reduce the heat to a simmer.

Carefully break one egg into each ring and poach gently for 5–6 minutes until set.

4 Meanwhile, cut the tomatoes into 8 thick slices and arrange on a piece of kitchen foil on the grill (broiler) rack. Grill (broil) for 2–3 minutes until just cooked. Season to taste.

5 Peel and thickly slice the mushrooms. Place in a saucepan with the stock, bring to the boil, cover and simmer for 4–5 minutes until cooked. Drain and keep warm.

6 To serve, arrange the tomato and mushroom slices on the toasted muffins and top each with 2 rashers of bacon. Carefully arrange an egg on top of each and sprinkle with a little pepper. Garnish with snipped fresh chives and serve at once.

VARIATION

Omit the bacon for a vegetarian version and use more tomatoes and mushrooms instead. Alternatively, include a grilled low-fat tofu or Quorn burger.

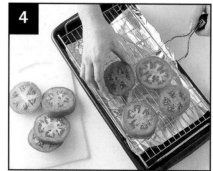

Cheesy Ham & Celery Savoury

Crisp celery wrapped in lean ham, topped with a light crust of cheese and spring onions (scallions), makes a delicious light lunch.

Serves 4

CALORIES PER SERVING: 155 • FAT CONTENT PER SERVING: 6.9 G

INGREDIENTS

4 sticks celery, with leaves
12 thin slices of lean ham
1 bunch spring onions (scallions)
175 g/6 oz low-fat soft cheese with
  garlic and herbs

6 tbsp low-fat natural (unsweetened)
  yogurt
4 tbsp Parmesan cheese, freshly
  grated
celery salt and pepper

TO SERVE:
tomato salad
crusty bread

1 Wash the celery, remove the leaves and reserve (if wished). Slice the celery sticks into 3 equal portions.

2 Cut any visible fat off the ham and lay the slices on a chopping board. Place a piece of celery on each piece of ham and roll up. Place 3 ham and celery rolls in each of 4 small, heatproof dishes.

3 Trim the spring onions (scallions), then finely shred both the white and green parts. Sprinkle the spring onions (scallions) over the ham and celery rolls and season with celery salt and pepper.

4 Mix together the soft cheese and yogurt and spoon over the ham and celery rolls.

5 Preheat the grill (broiler) to medium. Sprinkle each portion with 1 tbsp grated Parmesan cheese and grill for 6–7 minutes until hot and the cheese has formed a crust. If the cheese starts to brown too quickly, lower the grill (broiler) setting slightly.

6 Serve immediately, garnished with chopped celery leaves (if using) and accompanied with a tomato salad and crusty bread.

COOK'S TIP

Parmesan is useful in low-fat recipes because its intense flavour means you need to use only a small amount.

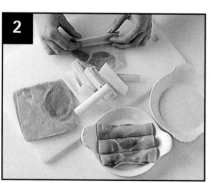

Parsleyed Chicken & Ham Pâté

*Pâté is easy to make at home, and this combination of lean chicken
and ham mixed with herbs is especially straightforward.*

Serves 4

CALORIES PER SERVING: 132 • FAT CONTENT PER SERVING: 1.8 G

INGREDIENTS

225 g/8 oz lean, skinless
   chicken, cooked
100 g/3¹/₂ oz lean ham, trimmed
small bunch fresh parsley
1 tsp lime rind, grated
2 tbsp lime juice

1 garlic clove, peeled
125 ml/4¹/₂ fl oz/¹/₂ cup low-fat
   natural fromage frais
   (unsweetened yogurt)
salt and pepper
1 tsp lime zest, to garnish

TO SERVE:
wedges of lime
crisp bread
green salad

1 Dice the chicken and ham and place in a blender or food processor. Add the parsley, lime rind and juice, and garlic and process well until finely minced. Alternatively, finely chop the chicken, ham, parsley and garlic and place in a bowl. Mix gently with the lime rind and juice.

2 Transfer the mixture to a bowl and mix in the fromage frais (yogurt). Season with salt and pepper to taste, cover and leave to chill in the refrigerator for about 30 minutes.

3 Pile the pâté into individual serving dishes and garnish with lime zest. Serve the pâtés with lime wedges, crisp bread and a fresh green salad.

VARIATION

This pâté can be made equally successfully with other kinds of minced, lean, cooked meat such as turkey, beef and pork. Alternatively, replace the chicken and ham with peeled prawns (shrimp) and/or white crab meat or with canned tuna in brine, drained. Remember that removing the skin from poultry reduces the fat content of any dish.

Spinach Cheese Moulds

These flavour-packed little moulds are a perfect starter or a tasty light lunch. Serve them with warm pitta bread.

Serves 4

<small>CALORIES PER SERVING: 64 • FAT CONTENT PER SERVING: 0.2 G</small>

INGREDIENTS

100 g/3^1/$_2$ oz fresh spinach leaves
300 g/10^1/$_2$ oz skimmed milk soft
  cheese
2 garlic cloves, crushed

sprigs of fresh parsley, tarragon and
  chives, finely chopped
salt and pepper

TO SERVE:
salad leaves and fresh herbs
pitta bread

1 Trim the stalks from the spinach leaves and rinse the leaves under running water. Pack the leaves into a saucepan while still wet, cover and cook for 3–4 minutes until wilted – they will cook in the steam from the wet leaves (do not overcook). Drain well and pat dry with absorbent kitchen paper.

2 Base-line 4 small pudding basins or individual ramekin dishes with baking parchment. Line the basins or ramekins with spinach leaves so that the leaves overhang the edges if they are large enough to do so.

3 Place the cheese in a bowl and add the garlic and herbs. Mix together thoroughly and season to taste.

4 Spoon the cheese and herb mixture into the basins or ramekins and pull over the overlapping spinach to cover the cheese, or lay extra leaves to cover the top. Place a greaseproof (waxed) paper circle on top of each dish and weigh down with a 100 g/3½ oz weight. Leave to chill in the refrigerator for 1 hour.

5 Remove the weights and peel off the paper. Loosen the moulds gently by running a small palette knife around the edges of each dish and turn them on to individual serving plates. Serve with a mixture of salad leaves and fresh herbs, and warm pitta bread.

Soufflé Omelette

The mouthwatering filling of sweet cherry tomatoes, mushrooms and peppery rocket (arugula) leaves is a wonderful contrast to the light fluffy omelettes, which have to be cooked one by one.

Serves 4

CALORIES PER SERVING: 141 • FAT CONTENT PER SERVING: 9.7 G

INGREDIENTS

175 g/6 oz cherry tomatoes
225 g/8 oz mixed mushrooms (such as button, chestnut, shiitake, oyster and wild mushrooms)

4 tbsp fresh vegetable stock
small bunch fresh thyme
4 medium eggs, separated
4 medium egg whites

4 tsp olive oil
25 g/1 oz rocket (arugula) leaves
salt and pepper
fresh thyme sprigs, to garnish

1 Halve the tomatoes and place them in a saucepan. Wipe the mushrooms with kitchen paper, trim if necessary and slice if large. Place in the saucepan.

2 Add the stock and thyme to the pan. Bring to the boil, cover and simmer for 5–6 minutes until tender. Drain, remove the thyme and discard, and keep the mixture warm.

3 Meanwhile, whisk the egg yolks with 8 tbsp water until frothy. In a clean, grease-free bowl, mix the 8 egg whites until stiff and dry.

4 Spoon the egg yolk mixture into the egg whites and, using a metal spoon, fold the whites and yolks into each other until well mixed. Take care not to knock out too much of the air.

5 For each omelette, brush a small omelette pan with 1 tsp oil and heat until hot. Pour in a quarter of the egg mixture and cook for 4–5 minutes until the mixture has set.

6 Preheat the grill (broiler) to medium and finish cooking the omelette for 2–3 minutes.

7 Transfer the omelette to a warm serving plate. Fill the omelette with a a few rocket (arugula) leaves, and a quarter of the mushroom and tomato mixture. Flip over the top of the omelette, garnish with sprigs of thyme and serve.

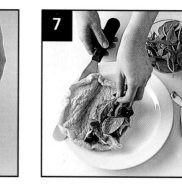

Grilled Rice & Tuna (Bell) Peppers

Grilled mixed sweet (bell) peppers are filled with tender tuna, sweetcorn,
nutty brown and wild rice and grated, reduced-fat Cheddar cheese.

Serves 4

CALORIES PER SERVING: 383 • FAT CONTENT PER SERVING: 6.8 G

INGREDIENTS

60 g/2 oz/^{1}/$_3$ cup wild rice
60 g/2 oz/^{1}/$_3$ cup brown rice
4 assorted medium (bell) peppers
200 g/7 oz can tuna fish in brine,
   drained and flaked

325 g/11^1/$_2$ oz can sweetcorn kernels
   (with no added sugar or salt),
   drained
100 g/3^1/$_2$ oz reduced-fat Cheddar
   cheese, grated
1 bunch fresh basil leaves, shredded

2 tbsp dry white breadcrumbs
1 tbsp Parmesan cheese,
   freshly grated
salt and pepper
fresh basil leaves, to garnish
crisp salad, to serve

1 Place the 2 rices in different saucepans, cover with water and cook according to the instructions on the packet. Drain well.

2 Meanwhile, preheat the grill (broiler) to medium. Halve the (bell) peppers, remove the seeds and stalks and arrange the peppers on the grill (broiler) rack, cut side down. Cook for 5 minutes, turn over and cook for a further 4–5 minutes.

3 Transfer the cooked rice to a mixing bowl and add the flaked tuna and drained sweetcorn. Gently fold in the grated cheese. Mix in the basil leaves and season to taste.

4 Divide the tuna and rice mixture into 8 equal portions. Pile each portion into each cooked (bell) pepper half. Mix together the breadcrumbs and Parmesan cheese and sprinkle over each (bell) pepper.

5 Place the (bell) peppers back under the grill (broiler) for 4–5 minutes until hot and golden-brown. Serve immediately, garnished with fresh basil leaves and accompanied with a fresh, crisp salad.

Baked Potatoes with a Spicy Filling

Crisp, twice-baked potatoes are partnered with an unusual filling of the Middle Eastern flavours of chickpeas (garbanzo beans), cumin and coriander.

Serves 4

CALORIES PER SERVING: 354 • FAT CONTENT PER SERVING: 5.9 G

INGREDIENTS

4 baking potatoes, each about
   300 g/10¹/₂ oz
1 tbsp vegetable oil
430 g/15¹/₂ oz can chickpeas
   (garbanzo beans), drained

1 tsp ground coriander
1 tsp ground cumin
4 tbsp fresh coriander (cilantro),
   chopped

150 ml/5 fl oz/²/₃ cup low-fat
   natural (unsweetened) yogurt
salt and pepper
salad, to serve

1 Preheat the oven to 200°C/400°F/Gas Mark 6. Scrub the potatoes and pat them dry in absorbent kitchen paper. Prick them all over with a fork, brush with oil and season.

2 Place the potatoes on a baking sheet and bake for 1–1¼ hours or until cooked through. Cool for 10 minutes.

3 Meanwhile, mash the chickpeas (garbanzo beans) with a fork or potato masher. Stir in the spices and half the chopped coriander (cilantro). Cover and set aside.

4 Halve the cooked potatoes and scoop the flesh into a bowl, keeping the shells intact. Mash the flesh until smooth and gently mix into the chickpea (garbanzo bean) mixture with the yogurt. Season well.

5 Place the potato shells on a baking sheet and fill with the potato and chickpea (garbanzo bean) mixture. Return the potatoes to the oven and bake for 10–15 minutes until heated through. Serve sprinkled with the remaining chopped coriander (cilantro) and a fresh salad made of chopped tomato, cucumber, coriander (cilantro) and red onion.

COOK'S TIP

For an even lower fat version of this recipe, bake the potatoes without oiling them first.

Spinach Crêpes with Curried Crab

Home-made crêpes are delicious and can be served with a variety of fillings. Here, white crab meat is lightly flavoured with curry spices and tossed in a low-fat dressing.

Serves 4

CALORIES PER SERVING: 259 • FAT CONTENT PER SERVING: 5.9 G

INGREDIENTS

115 g/4 oz buckwheat flour
1 large egg, beaten
300 ml/^{1}/$_2$ pint/1^1/$_4$ cups
   skimmed milk
125 g/4^1/$_2$ oz frozen spinach,
   thawed, well-drained and chopped
2 tsp vegetable oil

FOR THE FILLING:
350 g/12 oz white crab meat
1 tsp mild curry powder
1 tbsp mango chutney
1 tbsp reduced-calorie mayonnaise
2 tbsp low-fat natural (unsweetened)
   yogurt

2 tbsp fresh coriander (cilantro),
   chopped

TO SERVE:
green salad
lemon wedges

1 Sift the flour into a bowl and remove any husks that remain in the sieve (strainer).

2 Make a well in the centre of the flour and add the egg. Gradually whisk in the milk, then blend in the spinach. Transfer the batter to a jug and allow to stand for 30 minutes.

3 To make the filling, mix together all the ingredients, except the coriander (cilantro), in a bowl, cover and chill until required.

4 Whisk the batter. Brush a small crêpe pan with a little oil, heat until hot and pour in enough batter to cover the base thinly. Cook for 1–2 minutes until set, turn over and cook for 1 minute until golden. Transfer to a warmed plate. Repeat to make 8 pancakes, layering them on the plate with baking parchment.

5 Stir the coriander (cilantro) into the crab mixture. Fold each pancake into quarters. Open one fold and fill with the crab mixture. Serve warm, with a green salad and lemon wedges.

VARIATION

Try lean diced chicken in a light white sauce or peeled prawns (shrimp) instead of the crab.

Meat & Poultry

The increased interest in healthy eating means that most supermarkets and butchers now offer special cuts of lean meat. Although they are often slightly more expensive than standard cuts, it is worth buying this meat and spending a little extra time cooking it carefully to enhance the flavour. You will not need to buy as much if you combine the meat with thoughtfully chosen and prepared vegetables.

Look out, too, for packs of low- or reduced-fat minced (ground) meat in your local supermarket, and include it in burgers or serve it in a flavour-filled sauce with rice or your favourite pasta.

Cut any visible fat from beef and pork before you cook it. Chicken and turkey are lower in fat than red meats, and you can make them even healthier by removing the skin. Duck is a rich meat with a distinctive flavour, and you need only a small amount to create apparently extravagant, flavourful dishes that are healthy, too.

Pan-cooked Pork with Fennel & Aniseed

Lean pork chops, stuffed with an aniseed and orange filling, are pan-cooked with fennel in an aniseed-flavoured sweet sauce.

Serves 4

CALORIES PER SERVING: 242 • FAT CONTENT PER SERVING: 6.4 G

INGREDIENTS

4 lean pork chops, 125 g/4¹/₂ oz each
60 g/2 oz/¹/₃ cup brown rice, cooked
1 tsp orange rind, grated
4 spring onions (scallions), trimmed
  and finely chopped
¹/₂ tsp aniseed

1 tbsp olive oil
1 fennel bulb, trimmed and thinly
  sliced
450 ml/16 fl oz/2 cups unsweetened
  orange juice
1 tbsp cornflour (cornstarch)

2 tbsp Pernod
salt and pepper
fennel fronds, to garnish
cooked vegetables, to serve

1 Trim away any excess fat from the pork chops. Using a small, sharp knife, make a slit in the centre of each chop to create a pocket.

2 Mix the rice, orange rind, spring onions (scallions), seasoning and aniseed together in a bowl. Press the mixture into the pocket of each chop, then press gently to seal.

3 Heat the oil in a frying pan (skillet) and fry the pork chops on each side for 2–3 minutes until lightly brown.

4 Add the sliced fennel and orange juice to the pan, bring to the boil and simmer for 15–20 minutes until the meat is tender and cooked through. Remove the pork and fennel with a slotted spoon and transfer to a serving plate.

5 Blend the cornflour (cornstarch) and Pernod together in a small bowl. Add the cornflour (cornstarch) mixture to the pan and stir into the pan juices. Cook for 2–3 minutes, stirring, until the sauce thickens.

6 Pour the Pernod sauce over the pork chops, garnish with fennel fronds and serve with a selection of cooked vegetables.

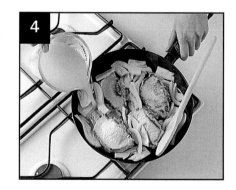

Pork Stroganoff

*Tender, lean pork, cooked in a rich tomato sauce with mushrooms and a green
(bell) pepper, is flavoured with the extra tang of natural (unsweetened) yogurt.*

Serves 4

CALORIES PER SERVING: 197 • FAT CONTENT PER SERVING: 7 G

INGREDIENTS

350 g/12 oz lean pork fillet
1 tbsp vegetable oil
1 medium onion, chopped
2 garlic cloves, crushed
25 g/1 oz plain (all-purpose) flour
2 tbsp tomato purée (paste)

425 ml/15 fl oz/1^{3}/$_{4}$ cups fresh
  chicken or vegetable stock
125 g/4^{1}/$_{2}$ oz button mushrooms,
  sliced
1 large green (bell) pepper, deseeded
  and diced
^{1}/$_{2}$ tsp ground nutmeg

4 tbsp low-fat natural (unsweetened)
  yogurt, plus extra to serve
salt and pepper
white rice, freshly boiled, to serve
ground nutmeg, to garnish

1 Trim away any excess fat and
silver skin from the pork,
then cut the meat into slices 1 cm/
^{1}/$_{2}$ inch thick.

2 Heat the oil in a large
saucepan and gently fry the
pork, onion and garlic for 4–5
minutes until lightly browned.

3 Stir in the flour and tomato
purée, pour in the stock and
stir to mix thoroughly.

4 Add the mushrooms, (bell)
pepper, seasoning and nutmeg.
Bring to the boil, cover and simmer
for 20 minutes until the pork is
tender and cooked through.

5 Remove the saucepan from
the heat and stir in the yogurt.

6 Serve the pork and sauce on a
bed of rice with an extra
spoonful of yogurt and garnish
with a dusting of ground nutmeg.

COOK'S TIP

*You can buy ready-made meat,
vegetable and fish stocks from
leading supermarkets. Although
more expensive they are better
nutritionally than stock cubes which
are high in salt and artificial
flavourings. Home-made stock
is best of all.*

Pan-cooked Pork Medallions with Apples & Cider

These lean and tender cuts of meat are thick slices cut from the fillet. In this dish they are perfectly complemented by eating (dessert) apples and dry (hard) cider.

Serves 4

CALORIES PER SERVING: 192 • FAT CONTENT PER SERVING: 5.7 G

INGREDIENTS

8 lean pork medallions, about
  50 g/1³/₄ oz each
2 tsp vegetable oil
1 medium onion, finely sliced
1 tsp caster (superfine) sugar

1 tsp dried sage
150 ml/5 fl oz/²/₃ cup dry (hard) cider
150 ml/5 fl oz/²/₃ cup fresh chicken
  or vegetable stock
1 green-skinned apple

1 red-skinned apple
1 tbsp lemon juice
salt and pepper
fresh sage leaves, to garnish
freshly cooked vegetables, to serve

1 Discard the string from the pork and trim away any excess fat. Re-tie with clean string and set aside.

2 Heat the oil in a frying pan (skillet) and gently fry the onion for 5 minutes until softened. Add the sugar and cook for 3–4 minutes until golden.

3 Add the pork to the pan and cook for 2 minutes on each side until browned. Add the sage, cider and stock. Bring to the boil and then simmer for 20 minutes.

4 Meanwhile, core and cut each apple into 8 wedges. Toss the apple wedges in lemon juice so that they do not turn brown.

5 Add the apples to the pork and mix gently. Season and cook for a further 3–4 minutes until tender.

6 Remove the string from the pork and serve immediately, garnished with fresh sage and accompanied with freshly cooked vegetables.

COOK'S TIP

If pork medallions are not available, buy 400g/14 oz pork fillet and slice it into evenly-sized medallions yourself.

Red Roast Pork with (Bell) Peppers

In this traditional Chinese dish the pork turns 'red' during cooking because it is basted in dark soy sauce. It is ideal served with sweet mixed (bell) peppers.

Serves 4

CALORIES PER SERVING: 282 • FAT CONTENT PER SERVING: 5 G

INGREDIENTS

450 g/1 lb lean pork fillets
6 tbsp dark soy sauce
2 tbsp dry sherry
1 tsp five-spice powder
2 garlic cloves, crushed (minced)

2.5 cm/1 inch piece root (fresh)
 ginger, finely chopped
1 large red (bell) pepper
1 large yellow (bell) pepper
1 large orange (bell) pepper

4 tbsp caster (superfine) sugar
2 tbsp red wine vinegar

TO GARNISH:
spring onions (scallions), shredded
fresh chives, snipped

1 Trim away excess fat and silver skin from the pork and place in a shallow dish.

2 Mix together the soy sauce, sherry, five-spice powder, garlic and ginger. Spoon over the pork, cover and marinate in the refrigerator for at least 1 hour.

3 Preheat the oven to 190°C/375°F/gas mark 5. Drain the pork, reserving the marinade. Place the pork on a roasting rack over a roasting pan.

Cook in the oven, occasionally basting with the marinade, for 1 hour or until cooked through.

4 Meanwhile, halve and deseed the (bell) peppers. Cut each (bell) pepper half into 3 equal portions. Arrange them on a baking sheet and bake alongside the pork for the last 30 minutes of cooking time.

5 Place the caster (superfine) sugar and vinegar in a small saucepan and heat gently until the

sugar dissolves. Bring to the boil and simmer for 3–4 minutes, until syrupy.

6 As soon as the pork is cooked, remove it from the oven and brush liberally with the sugar syrup. Allow to stand for about 5 minutes, then slice and arrange on a warm serving platter with the (bell) peppers.

7 Serve garnished with the spring onions (scallions) and freshly snipped chives.

Pork with Ratatouille Sauce

*Serve this delicious combination of meat and vegetables
with baked potatoes for an appetizing supper dish.*

Serves 4

CALORIES PER SERVING: 214 • FAT CONTENT PER SERVING: 5.6 G

INGREDIENTS

4 lean, boneless pork chops, about
125 g/4^1/$_2$ oz each
1 tsp dried mixed herbs
salt and pepper
baked potatoes, to serve

SAUCE:
1 medium onion
1 garlic clove
1 small green (bell) pepper
1 small yellow (bell) pepper
1 medium courgette (zucchini)

100 g/3^1/$_2$ oz button mushrooms
400 g/14 oz can chopped tomatoes
2 tbsp tomato purée (paste)
1 tsp dried mixed herbs
1 tsp caster (superfine) sugar

1 To make the sauce, peel and chop the onion and garlic. Deseed and dice the (bell) peppers. Trim and dice the courgette (zucchini). Wipe and halve the mushrooms.

2 Place all of the vegetables in a saucepan and stir in the chopped tomatoes and tomato purée (paste). Add the dried herbs, sugar and plenty of seasoning. Bring to the boil, cover and simmer for 20 minutes.

3 Meanwhile, preheat the grill (broiler) to medium. Trim away any excess fat from the chops, then season on both sides and rub in the dried mixed herbs. Cook the chops for 5 minutes, then turn over and cook for a further 6–7 minutes until cooked through.

4 Drain the chops on absorbent kitchen paper and serve accompanied with the sauce and baked potatoes.

COOK'S TIP

This vegetable sauce could be served with any other grilled (broiled) or baked meat or fish. It would also make an excellent alternative filling for the Spinach Crêpes on page 46.

Beef & Orange Curry

A citrusy, spicy blend of tender chunks of tender beef with the tang of orange and the warmth of Indian spices. For a well-balanced meal, serve with boiled rice and a cucumber raita.

Serves 4

CALORIES PER SERVING: 283 • FAT CONTENT PER SERVING: 10.5 G

INGREDIENTS

1 tbsp vegetable oil
225 g/8 oz shallots, halved
2 garlic cloves, crushed (minced)
450 g/1 lb lean rump or sirloin beef, trimmed and cut into 2 cm/ ³/4 inch cubes
3 tbsp curry paste

450 ml/16 fl oz/2 cups fresh beef stock
4 medium oranges
2 tsp cornflour (cornstarch)
salt and pepper
2 tbsp fresh coriander (cilantro), chopped, to garnish

Basmati rice, freshly boiled, to serve

RAITA:
¹/2 cucumber, finely diced
3 tbsp fresh mint, chopped
150 ml/5 fl oz/²/3 cup low-fat natural (unsweetened) yogurt

1 Heat the oil in a large saucepan. Gently fry the shallots, garlic and the cubes of beef for 5 minutes, stirring occasionally, until the beef is evenly browned all over.

2 Blend together the curry paste and stock. Add the mixture to the beef and stir to mix thoroughly. Bring to the boil, cover and simmer for 1 hour or until the meat is tender.

3 Meanwhile, grate the rind of one orange. Extract the juice from the orange and from a second orange. Peel the two remaining oranges, removing as much pith as possible. Slice between each segment and remove the flesh.

4 Blend the cornflour (cornstarch) with the orange juice. At the end of the cooking time, stir the orange rind into the beef along with the orange and

cornflour (cornstarch) mixture. Bring to the boil and simmer, stirring, for 3–4 minutes until the sauce thickens. Season to taste and stir in the orange segments.

5 To make the raita, mix the cucumber with the mint and stir in the yogurt. Season with salt and pepper to taste.

6 Serve the curry with rice and the cucumber raita.

Pan-seared Beef with Ginger, Pineapple & Chilli

Serve these fruity, hot and spicy steaks with noodles. Use a non-stick, ridged frying pan (skillet) for the best results – it will help you cook with a minimum of fat.

Serves 4

CALORIES PER SERVING: 191 • FAT CONTENT PER SERVING: 5.1 G

INGREDIENTS

4 lean beef steaks (such as rump, sirloin or fillet), 100 g/3¹/₂ oz each
2 tbsp ginger wine
2.5 cm/1 inch piece root (fresh) ginger, finely chopped
1 garlic clove, crushed (minced)
1 tsp ground chilli

1 tsp vegetable oil
red chilli strips, to garnish
salt and pepper

TO SERVE:
freshly cooked noodles
2 spring onions (scallions), shredded

RELISH:
225 g/8 oz fresh pineapple
1 small red (bell) pepper
1 red chilli
2 tbsp light soy sauce
1 piece stem ginger in syrup, drained and chopped

1 Trim any excess fat from the beef if necessary. Using a meat mallet or covered rolling pin, pound the steaks until 1 cm/¹/₂ inch thick. Season on both sides and place in a shallow dish.

2 Mix the ginger wine, root (fresh) ginger, garlic and chilli and pour over the meat. Cover and chill for 30 minutes.

3 Meanwhile, make the relish. Peel and finely chop the pineapple and place it in a bowl. Halve, deseed and finely chop the (bell) pepper and chilli. Stir into the pineapple together with the soy sauce and stem ginger. Cover and chill until required.

4 Brush a non-stick frying pan (skillet) with the oil and heat until very hot. Drain the beef and add to the pan, pressing down to seal. Lower the heat and cook for 5 minutes. Turn the steaks over and cook for a further 5 minutes.

5 Drain the steaks on kitchen paper and transfer to serving plates. Garnish with chilli strips, and serve with noodles, spring onions (scallions) and the relish.

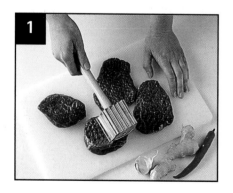

Beef & Tomato Gratin

*A satisfying bake of lean minced beef, courgettes (zucchini)
and tomatoes cooked in a low-fat 'custard' with a cheesy crust.*

Serves 4

CALORIES PER SERVING: 319 • FAT CONTENT PER SERVING: 10.3 G

INGREDIENTS

350 g/12 oz lean beef, minced
  (ground)
1 large onion, finely chopped
1 tsp dried mixed herbs
1 tbsp plain (all-purpose) flour
300 ml/$\frac{1}{2}$ pint/1$\frac{1}{4}$ cups beef stock
1 tbsp tomato purée (paste)
2 large tomatoes, thinly sliced

4 medium courgettes (zucchini),
  thinly sliced
2 tbsp cornflour (cornstarch)
300 ml/$\frac{1}{2}$ pint/1$\frac{1}{4}$ cups skimmed
  milk
150 ml/5 fl oz/$\frac{2}{3}$ cup low-fat
  natural fromage frais
  (unsweetened yogurt)

1 medium egg yolk
4 tbsp Parmesan cheese, freshly
  grated
salt and pepper

TO SERVE:
crusty bread
steamed vegetables

1 Preheat the oven to 190°C/
375°F/Gas Mark 5. In a large
pan, dry-fry the beef and onion
for 4–5 minutes until browned.

2 Stir in the herbs, flour, stock
and tomato purée (paste), and
season. Bring to a boil and simmer
for 30 minutes until thickened.

3 Transfer the beef mixture to
an ovenproof gratin dish.

Cover with a layer of the sliced
tomatoes and then add a layer of
sliced courgettes (zucchini). Set
aside until required.

4 Blend the cornflour
(cornstarch) with a little milk
in a small bowl. Pour the
remaining milk into a saucepan
and bring to the boil. Add the
cornflour (cornstarch) mixture
and cook, stirring, for 1–2 minutes

until thickened. Remove from the
heat and beat in the fromage frais
(yogurt) and egg yolk. Season well.

5 Spread the white sauce over
the layer of courgettes
(zucchini). Place the dish on to a
baking sheet and sprinkle with
grated Parmesan. Bake in the oven
for 25–30 minutes until golden-
brown. Serve with crusty bread
and steamed vegetables.

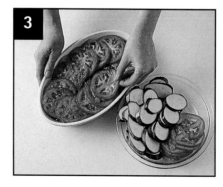

Sweet & Sour Venison Stir-fry

*Venison is super-lean and low in fat, so it's the perfect choice for
a low-fat diet. Cooked quickly with crisp vegetables, it's ideal in a stir-fry.*

Serves 4

CALORIES PER SERVING: 174 • FAT CONTENT PER SERVING: 1.9 G

INGREDIENTS

1 bunch spring onions (scallion)
1 red (bell) pepper
100 g/3¹/₂ oz mangetout (snow peas)
100 g/3¹/₂ oz baby sweetcorn
350 g/12 oz lean venison steak
1 tbsp vegetable oil

1 clove garlic, crushed (minced)
2.5 cm/1 inch piece root (fresh)
  ginger, finely chopped
3 tbsp light soy sauce, plus extra
  for serving
1 tbsp white wine vinegar

2 tbsp dry sherry
2 tsp clear honey
225 g/8 oz can pineapple pieces in
  natural juice, drained
25 g/1 oz beansprouts
freshly cooked rice, to serve

1 Trim the spring onions (scallions) and cut into 2.5 cm/1 inch pieces. Halve and deseed the (bell) pepper and cut it into 2.5 cm/1 inch pieces. Top and tail the mangetout (snow peas) and trim the baby corn.

2 Trim the excess fat from the meat and cut it into thin strips. Heat the oil in a large frying pan (skillet) or wok until hot and stir-fry the meat, garlic and ginger for 5 minutes.

3 Add the prepared spring onion (scallion), (bell) pepper, mangetout (snow peas) and baby corn to the pan, then add the soy sauce, vinegar, sherry and honey. Stir-fry for a further 5 minutes, keeping the heat high.

4 Carefully stir in the pineapple pieces and beansprouts and cook for a further 1–2 minutes to heat through. Serve with freshly cooked rice and extra soy sauce for dipping.

VARIATION

For a quick and nutritious meal-in-one, cook 225 g/8 oz egg noodles in boiling water for 3–4 minutes. Drain well and add to the pan in step 4, together with the pineapple and beansprouts. Stir well to mix. You will have to add an extra 2 tbsp soy sauce with the pineapple and beansprouts so that the stir-fry does not dry out.

Venison & Garlic Mash

Rich game is best served with a sweet fruit sauce. These small tender steaks of venison are cooked with sweet, juicy prunes and redcurrant jelly.

Serves 4

<small>CALORIES PER SERVING: 503 • FAT CONTENT PER SERVING: 6.1 G</small>

INGREDIENTS

8 medallions of venison, 75 g/2³/₄ oz each

1 tbsp vegetable oil

1 red onion, chopped

150 ml/5 fl oz/²/₃ cup fresh beef stock

150 ml/5 fl oz/²/₃ cup red wine

3 tbsp redcurrant jelly

100 g/3¹/₂ oz no-need-to-soak dried, pitted prunes

2 tsp cornflour (cornstarch)

2 tbsp brandy

salt and pepper

patty pans, to serve (optional)

GARLIC MASH:

900 g/2 lb potatoes, peeled and diced

¹/₂ tsp garlic purée (paste)

2 tbsp low-fat natural fromage frais (unsweetened yogurt)

4 tbsp fresh parsley, chopped

1 Trim off any excess fat from the meat and season with salt and pepper on both sides.

2 Heat the oil in a frying pan (skillet) and fry the medallions with the onions on a high heat for 2 minutes on each side until brown.

3 Lower the heat and pour in the stock and wine. Add the redcurrant jelly and prunes and stir until the jelly melts. Bring to

the boil, cover and simmer for 10 minutes until cooked through.

4 Meanwhile, make the garlic mash. Place the potatoes in a saucepan and cover with water. Bring to the boil and cook for 8–10 minutes until tender. Drain well.

5 Mash the potatoes until smooth. Add the garlic purée (paste), fromage frais (yogurt) and parsley and blend thoroughly. Season, set aside and keep warm.

6 Remove the medallions from the frying pan (skillet) with a slotted spoon and keep warm.

7 Blend the cornflour (cornstarch) with the brandy in a small bowl and add to the pan juices. Heat, stirring, until thickened. Season with salt and pepper to taste.

8 Serve the venison with the redcurrant and prune sauce and garlic mash.

Venison Meatballs with Sherried Kumquat Sauce

The sharp, citrusy flavour of kumquats is the perfect complement to these tasty steamed meatballs. Serve simply on a bed of pasta or noodles with some fresh vegetables.

Serves 4

CALORIES PER SERVING: 178 • FAT CONTENT PER SERVING: 2.1 G

INGREDIENTS

450 g/1 lb lean venison, minced (ground)

1 small leek, finely chopped

1 medium carrot, finely grated

$^1/_2$ tsp ground nutmeg

1 medium egg white, lightly beaten

salt and pepper

TO SERVE:

freshly cooked pasta or noodles

freshly cooked vegetables

SAUCE:

100 g/3$^1/_2$ oz kumquats

15 g/$^1/_2$ oz caster (superfine) sugar

150 ml/5 fl oz/$^2/_3$ cup water

4 tbsp dry sherry

1 tsp cornflour (cornstarch)

1 Place the venison in a mixing bowl together with the leek, carrot, seasoning and nutmeg. Add the egg white and bind the ingredients together with your hands until the mixture is well moulded and firm.

2 Divide the mixture into 16 equal portions. Using your fingers, form each portion into a small round ball.

3 Bring a large saucepan of water to the boil. Arrange the meatballs on a layer of baking parchment in a steamer or large sieve (strainer) and place over the boiling water. Cover and steam for 10 minutes until cooked through.

4 Meanwhile, make the sauce. Wash and thinly slice the kumquats. Place them in a saucepan with the sugar and water

and bring to the boil. Simmer for 2–3 minutes until tender.

5 Blend the sherry and cornflour (cornstarch) together and add to the pan. Heat through, stirring, until the sauce thickens. Season.

6 Drain the meatballs and transfer to a serving plate. Spoon over the sauce and serve with pasta and vegetables.

Fruity Lamb Casserole

The sweet spicy blend of cinnamon, coriander and cumin is the perfect foil for the tender lamb and apricots in this warming casserole

Serves 4

CALORIES PER SERVING: 280 • FAT CONTENT PER SERVING: 11.6 G

INGREDIENTS

450 g/1 lb lean lamb, trimmed and cut into 2.5 cm/1 inch cubes
1 tsp ground cinnamon
1 tsp ground coriander
1 tsp ground cumin
2 tsp olive oil
1 medium red onion, finely chopped

1 garlic clove, crushed
400 g/14 oz can chopped tomatoes
2 tbsp tomato purée (paste)
125 g/4$^1/_2$ oz no-soak dried apricots
1 tsp caster (superfine) sugar
300 ml/$^1/_2$ pint/1$^1/_4$ cups vegetable stock

salt and pepper
1 small bunch fresh coriander (cilantro), to garnish
brown rice, steamed couscous or bulgar wheat, to serve

1 Preheat the oven to 180°C/350°F/gas mark 4. Place the meat in a mixing bowl and add the spices and oil. Mix thoroughly so that the lamb is coated in the spices.

2 Heat a non-stick frying pan (skillet) for a few seconds until it is hot, then add the spiced lamb. Reduce the heat and cook for 4–5 minutes, stirring, until browned all over. Using a slotted spoon, remove the lamb and transfer to a large ovenproof casserole.

3 In the same frying pan (skillet), cook the onion, garlic, tomatoes and tomato purée (paste) for 5 minutes. Season to taste. Stir in the apricots and sugar, add the stock and bring to the boil.

4 Spoon the sauce over the lamb and mix well. Cover and cook in the oven for 1 hour, removing the lid for the last 10 minutes.

5 Roughly chop the coriander (cilantro) and sprinkle over the casserole to garnish. Serve with brown rice, steamed couscous or bulgar wheat.

Lamb, (Bell) Pepper & Couscous

Couscous is a dish that originated among the Berbers, and it is a staple of North Africa. When it is steamed, it is a delicious plump grain, ideal for serving with a stew.

Serves 4

CALORIES PER SERVING: 522 • FAT CONTENT PER SERVING: 12.5 G

INGREDIENTS

2 medium red onions, sliced

juice of 1 lemon

1 large red (bell) pepper, deseeded and thickly sliced

1 large green (bell) pepper, deseeded and thickly sliced

1 large orange (bell) pepper, deseeded and thickly sliced

pinch of saffron strands

cinnamon stick, broken

1 tbsp clear honey

300 ml/½ pint/1¼ cups vegetable stock

2 tsp olive oil

350 g/12 oz lean lamb fillet, trimmed and sliced

1 tsp Harissa paste

200 g/7 oz can chopped tomatoes

425 g/15 oz can chickpeas (garbanzo beans), drained

350 g/12 oz precooked couscous

2 tsp ground cinnamon

salt and pepper

1 Toss the onions in the lemon juice and transfer to a saucepan. Mix in the (bell) peppers, saffron, cinnamon stick and honey. Pour in the stock, bring to the boil, cover and simmer for 5 minutes.

2 Meanwhile, heat the oil in a frying pan (skillet) and gently fry the lamb for 3–4 minutes until browned all over.

3 Using a slotted spoon, drain the lamb and transfer it to the pan with the onions and peppers. Season and stir in the Harissa paste, tomatoes and chickpeas (garbanzo beans). Mix well, bring back to the boil and simmer, uncovered, for 20 minutes.

4 Meanwhile, soak the couscous, following the instructions on the packet. Bring a saucepan of water to the boil. Transfer the couscous to a steamer or sieve (strainer) lined with muslin (cheesecloth) and place over the pan of boiling water. Cover and steam as directed.

5 Transfer the couscous to a warm serving platter and dust with ground cinnamon. Discard the cinnamon stick and spoon the stew over the couscous to serve.

Hot Pot Chops

A Hot Pot is a lamb casserole, made with carrots and onions and with a potato topping, that is traditionally made in the North of England. The chops used here are an interesting alternative.

Serves 4

CALORIES PER SERVING: 252 • FAT CONTENT PER SERVING: 11.3 G

INGREDIENTS

4 lean, boneless lamb leg steaks, about 125 g/4^1/$_2$ oz each
1 small onion, thinly sliced
1 medium carrot, thinly sliced
1 medium potato, thinly sliced

1 tsp olive oil
1 tsp dried rosemary
salt and pepper
fresh rosemary, to garnish

freshly steamed green vegetables, to serve

1 Preheat the oven to 180°C/ 350°F/gas mark 4. Using a sharp knife, trim any excess fat from the lamb steaks.

2 Season both sides of the steaks with salt and pepper and arrange them on a baking tray.

3 Alternate layers of sliced onion, carrot and potato on top of each lamb steak.

4 Brush the tops of the potato lightly with oil, season well with salt and pepper to taste and then sprinkle with a little dried rosemary.

5 Bake the hot pot chops in the oven for 25–30 minutes until the lamb is tender and cooked through.

6 Drain the lamb on absorbent kitchen paper and transfer to a warmed serving plate. Garnish with fresh rosemary and serve accompanied with a selection of green vegetables.

VARIATION

This recipe would work equally well with boneless chicken breasts. Pound the chicken slightly with a meat mallet or covered rolling pin so that the pieces are the same thickness throughout.

Minty Lamb Burgers

A tasty alternative to traditional hamburgers, these lamb burgers are
flavoured with mint and are accompanied with a smooth minty dressing.

Serves 4

CALORIES PER SERVING: 237 • FAT CONTENT PER SERVING: 7.8 G

INGREDIENTS

350 g/12 oz lean lamb, minced
  (ground)
1 medium onion, finely chopped
4 tbsp dry wholemeal breadcrumbs
2 tbsp mint jelly
salt and pepper

TO SERVE:
4 wholemeal baps, split
2 large tomatoes, sliced
small piece of cucumber, sliced
lettuce leaves

RELISH:
4 tbsp low-fat natural fromage frais
  (unsweetened yogurt)
1 tbsp mint jelly, softened
5 cm/2 inch piece of cucumber, finely
  diced
1 tbsp fresh mint, chopped

1 Place the lamb in a large bowl and mix in the onion, breadcrumbs and jelly. Season well, then mould the ingredients together with your hands to form a firm mixture.

2 Divide the mixture into 4 and shape each portion into a round measuring 10 cm/4 inches across. Place the rounds on a plate lined with baking parchment and leave to chill for 30 minutes.

3 Preheat the grill (broiler) to medium. Line a grill rack with baking parchment, securing the ends under the rack, and place the burgers on top. Cook for 8 minutes, then turn over the burgers and cook for a further 7 minutes or until cooked through.

4 Meanwhile, make the relish. Mix together the fromage frais (unsweetened yogurt), mint jelly, cucumber and freshly chopped mint in a bowl. Cover and leave to chill in the refrigerator until required.

5 Drain the burgers on absorbent kitchen paper. Serve the burgers inside the baps and top with sliced tomatoes, cucumber, lettuce and relish.

Tricolour Chicken & Spinach Lasagne

A delicious pasta bake that is filled with the colours of the Italian flag – red from the tomatoes, green from the spinach and pasta, and white from the chicken and the sauce.

Serves 4

CALORIES PER SERVING: 424 • FAT CONTENT PER SERVING: 7.2 G

INGREDIENTS

350 g/12 oz frozen chopped spinach, thawed and drained

$1/2$ tsp ground nutmeg

450 g/1 lb lean, cooked chicken meat, skinned and diced

4 sheets no-pre-cook lasagne verde

$1^1/2$ tbsp cornflour (cornstarch)

425 ml/15 fl oz/$1^3/4$ cups skimmed milk

4 tbsp Parmesan cheese, freshly grated

salt and pepper

freshly prepared salad, to serve

TOMATO SAUCE:

400 g/14 oz can chopped tomatoes

1 medium onion, finely chopped

1 garlic clove, crushed (minced)

150 ml/5 fl oz/$2/3$ cup white wine

3 tbsp tomato purée (paste)

1 tsp dried oregano

1 Preheat the oven to 200°C/ 400°F/Gas Mark 6. To make the tomato sauce, place the tomatoes in a saucepan and stir in the onion, garlic, wine, tomato purée (paste) and oregano. Bring to the boil and simmer for 20 minutes until thick. Season well.

2 Drain the spinach again and spread it out on absorbent kitchen paper to make sure that as much water as possible has been removed. Layer the spinach in the base of an ovenproof baking dish. Sprinkle with nutmeg and season.

3 Arrange the diced chicken over the spinach and spoon over the tomato sauce. Arrange the sheets of lasagne over the tomato sauce.

4 Blend the cornflour (cornstarch) with a little of the milk to make a paste. Pour the remaining milk into a saucepan and stir in the cornflour (cornstarch) paste. Heat for 2–3 minutes, stirring, until the sauce thickens. Season well.

5 Spoon the sauce over the lasagne and transfer the dish to a baking sheet. Sprinkle the grated cheese over the sauce and bake in the oven for 25 minutes until golden-brown. Serve with a fresh green salad.

Chicken Pasta Bake with Fennel & Raisins

Tender lean chicken is baked with pasta quills in a creamy, low-fat cheese sauce with a hint of aniseed and the sweetness of juicy raisins.

Serves 4

CALORIES PER SERVING: 521 • FAT CONTENT PER SERVING: 15.5 G

INGREDIENTS

2 bulbs fennel
2 medium red onions, finely shredded
1 tbsp lemon juice
125 g/4^{1}/2 oz button mushrooms
1 tbsp olive oil

225 g/8 oz penne (quills)
60 g/2 oz/^{1}/3 cup raisins
225 g/8 oz lean, boneless cooked chicken, skinned and shredded
375 g/13 oz low-fat soft cheese with garlic and herbs

125 g/4^{1}/2 oz low-fat Mozzarella cheese, thinly sliced
2 tbsp Parmesan cheese, grated
salt and pepper

1 Preheat the oven to 200°C/ 400°F/Gas Mark 6. Trim the fennel, reserving the green fronds for garnishing, and slice the bulbs thinly. Generously coat the onion in the lemon juice. Quarter the mushrooms.

2 Heat the oil in a large frying pan (skillet) and fry the fennel, onion and mushrooms for 4–5 minutes, stirring, until just softened. Season well, transfer the vegetable mixture to a large mixing bowl and set aside.

3 Bring a pan of lightly salted water to the boil and cook the penne (quills) according to the instructions on the packet until *al dente* (just cooked). Drain and mix the pasta with the vegetables.

4 Stir the raisins and chicken into the pasta mixture. Soften the soft cheese by beating it, then mix into the pasta and chicken – the heat from the pasta should make the cheese melt slightly.

5 Put the mixture into an ovenproof baking dish and transfer to a baking sheet. Arrange slices of Mozzarella cheese over the top and sprinkle with the grated Parmesan. Bake in the oven for 20–25 minutes until golden-brown. Garnish with chopped fennel fronds and serve hot.

Baked Southern-style Chicken & Chips

Traditionally, this dish is deep-fried, but the low-fat version is just as mouthwatering. Serve with chunky potato wedge chips for a really authentic meal.

Serves 4

CALORIES PER SERVING: 402 • FAT CONTENT PER SERVING: 7.4 G

INGREDIENTS

4 baking potatoes, each 225 g/8 oz
1 tbsp sunflower oil
2 tsp coarse sea salt
2 tbsp plain (all-purpose) flour
pinch of cayenne pepper

$^1/_2$ tsp paprika pepper
$^1/_2$ tsp dried thyme
8 chicken drumsticks, skin removed
1 medium egg, beaten
2 tbsp cold water

6 tbsp dry white breadcrumbs
salt and pepper

TO SERVE:
low-fat coleslaw salad
sweetcorn relish

1 Preheat the oven to 200°C/ 400°F/Gas Mark 6. Wash and scrub the potatoes and cut each into 8 equal portions. Place in a clean plastic bag and add the oil. Seal and shake well to coat.

2 Arrange the potato wedges, skin side down, on a non-stick baking sheet, sprinkle over the sea salt and bake in the oven for 30–35 minutes until they are tender and golden.

3 Meanwhile, mix the flour, spices, thyme and seasoning together on a plate. Press the chicken drumsticks into the seasoned flour to lightly coat.

4 On one plate mix together the egg and water. On another plate sprinkle the breadcrumbs. Dip the chicken drumsticks first in the egg and then in the breadcrumbs. Place on a non-stick baking sheet.

5 Bake the chicken drumsticks alongside the potato wedges for 30 minutes, turning after 15 minutes, until they are tender and cooked through.

6 Drain the potato wedges thoroughly on absorbent kitchen paper to remove any excess fat and serve with the chicken, accompanied with low-fat coleslaw and sweetcorn relish, if wished.

Lime Chicken Skewers with Mango Salsa

These succulent chicken kebabs (kabobs) are coated in a sweet lime dressing and are best served with a lime and mango relish. They make a refreshing light meal.

Serves 4

CALORIES PER SERVING: 200 • FAT CONTENT PER SERVING: 1.5 G

INGREDIENTS

4 boneless chicken breasts, skinned, about 125 g/4$^{1}/_{2}$ oz each
3 tbsp lime marmalade
1 tsp white wine vinegar
$^{1}/_{2}$ tsp lime rind, finely grated
1 tbsp lime juice

salt and pepper

TO SERVE:
lime wedges
boiled white rice, sprinkled with chilli powder

SALSA:
1 small mango
1 small red onion
1 tbsp lime juice
1 tbsp fresh coriander (cilantro), chopped

1 Slice the chicken breasts into thin pieces and thread on to 8 skewers so that the meat forms an S-shape down each skewer.

2 Preheat the grill (broiler) to medium. Arrange the chicken skewers on the grill (broiler) rack. Mix together the marmalade, vinegar, lime rind and juice. Season with salt and pepper to taste. Brush the dressing generously over the chicken and grill for 5 minutes. Turn the chicken over, brush with the dressing again and grill for a further 4-5 minutes until the chicken is cooked through.

3 Meanwhile, prepare the salsa. Peel the mango and slice the flesh off the smooth, central stone. Dice the flesh into small pieces and place in a small bowl.

4 Peel and finely chop the onion and mix into the mango, together with the lime juice and chopped coriander (cilantro). Season, cover and chill until required.

5 Serve the chicken kebabs (kabobs) with the salsa, accompanied with wedges of lime and boiled rice sprinkled with chilli powder.

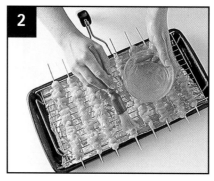

Sage Chicken & Rice

Cooking in a single pot means that all of the flavours are retained.
This is a substantial meal that needs only a salad and some crusty bread.

Serves 4

CALORIES PER SERVING: 391 • FAT CONTENT PER SERVING: 3.9 G

INGREDIENTS

1 large onion, chopped
1 garlic clove, crushed (minced)
2 sticks celery, sliced
2 carrots, diced
2 sprigs fresh sage
300 ml/½ pint/1¼ cups chicken stock
350 g/12 oz boneless, skinless
   chicken breasts

225 g/8 oz/1⅓ cups mixed brown
   and wild rice
400 g/14 oz can chopped tomatoes
dash of Tabasco sauce
2 medium courgettes (zucchini),
   trimmed and thinly sliced
100 g/3½ oz lean ham, diced
salt and pepper

fresh sage, to garnish

TO SERVE:
salad leaves
crusty bread

1 Place the onion, garlic, celery, carrots and sprigs of fresh sage in a large saucepan and pour in the chicken stock. Bring to the boil, cover the pan and simmer for 5 minutes.

2 Cut the chicken into 2.5 cm/ 1 inch cubes and stir into the pan with the vegetables. Cover the pan and continue to cook for a further 5 minutes.

3 Stir in the rice and chopped tomatoes. Add a dash of Tabasco sauce to taste and season well. Bring to the boil, cover and simmer for 25 minutes.

4 Stir in the sliced courgettes (zucchini) and diced ham and continue to cook, uncovered, for a further 10 minutes, stirring occasionally, until the rice is just tender.

5 Remove and discard the sprigs of sage. Garnish with a few sage leaves and serve with a fresh salad and crusty bread.

COOK'S TIP

If you do not have fresh sage, use 1 tsp of dried sage in step 1.

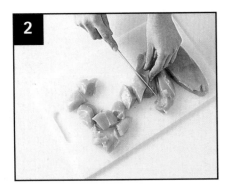

Chilli Chicken & Sweetcorn Meatballs

Tender chicken nuggets are served with a sweet and sour sauce.

Serves 4

Calories per serving: 223 • Fat content per serving: 3 g

INGREDIENTS

450 g/1 lb lean chicken, minced (ground)

4 spring onions (scallions), trimmed and finely chopped

1 small red chilli, deseeded and finely chopped

2.5 cm/1 inch piece root (fresh) ginger, finely chopped

100 g/3½ oz can sweetcorn (no added sugar or salt), drained

salt and white pepper

TO SERVE:

boiled jasmine rice

chives, snipped

SAUCE:

150 ml/5 fl oz/²/₃ cup fresh chicken stock

100 g/3½ oz cubed pineapple in natural juice, drained, with 4 tbsp reserved juice

1 medium carrot, cut into thin strips

1 small red (bell) pepper, deseeded and diced

1 small green (bell) pepper, deseeded and diced

1 tbsp light soy sauce

2 tbsp rice vinegar

1 tbsp caster (superfine) sugar

1 tbsp tomato purée (paste)

2 tsp cornflour (cornstarch) mixed to a paste with 4 tsp cold water

1 To make the meatballs, place the chicken in a bowl and add the spring onions (scallion), chilli, ginger, seasoning and sweetcorn. Mix together with your hands.

2 Divide the mixture into 16 portions and form each into a ball. Bring a saucepan of water to the boil. Arrange the meatballs on a sheet of baking parchment in a steamer or large sieve (strainer), place over the water, cover and steam for 10–12 minutes.

3 To make the sauce, pour the stock and pineapple juice into a saucepan and bring to the boil. Add the carrot and (bell) peppers, cover and simmer for 5 minutes.

4 Stir in the remaining ingredients and heat through, stirring, until thickened. Season and set aside until required.

5 Drain the meatballs and transfer to a serving plate. Garnish with snipped chives and serve with boiled rice and the sauce (re-heated if necessary).

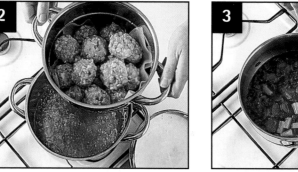

Crispy-Topped Stuffed Chicken

An attractive main course of chicken breasts filled with mixed (bell) peppers and set on a sea of red (bell) peppers and tomato sauce.

Serves 4

CALORIES PER SERVING: 211 • FAT CONTENT PER SERVING: 3.8 G

INGREDIENTS

4 boneless chicken breasts, about 150 g/5^1/$_2$ oz each, skinned

4 sprigs fresh tarragon

^{1}/$_2$ small orange (bell) pepper, deseeded and sliced

^{1}/$_2$ small green (bell) pepper, deseeded and sliced

15 g/^{1}/$_2$ oz wholemeal breadcrumbs

1 tbsp sesame seeds

4 tbsp lemon juice

1 small red (bell) pepper, halved and deseeded

200 g/7 oz can chopped tomatoes

1 small red chilli, deseeded and chopped

^{1}/$_4$ tsp celery salt

salt and pepper

fresh tarragon, to garnish

1 Preheat the oven to 200°C/ 400°F/Gas Mark 6. Slit the chicken breasts with a small, sharp knife to create a pocket in each. Season inside each pocket.

2 Place a sprig of tarragon and a few slices of orange and green (bell) peppers in each pocket. Place the chicken breasts on a non-stick baking sheet and sprinkle over the breadcrumbs and sesame seeds.

3 Spoon 1 tbsp lemon juice over each chicken breast and bake in the oven for 35–40 minutes until the chicken is tender and cooked through.

4 Meanwhile, preheat the grill (broiler) to hot. Arrange the red (bell) pepper halves, skin side up, on the rack and cook for 5–6 minutes until the skin blisters. Leave to cool for 10 minutes, then peel off the skins.

5 Put the red (bell) pepper in a blender, add the tomatoes, chilli and celery salt and process for a few seconds. Season to taste. Alternatively, finely chop the red (bell) pepper and rub through a sieve with the tomatoes and chilli.

6 When the chicken is cooked, heat the sauce, spoon a little on to a warm plate and arrange a chicken breast in the centre. Garnish with tarragon and serve.

Chicken with a Curried Yogurt Crust

A spicy, Indian-style coating is baked around lean chicken to give a full flavour.
Serve hot or cold with a tomato, cucumber and coriander (cilantro) relish.

Serves 4

CALORIES PER SERVING: 176 • FAT CONTENT PER SERVING: 2 G

INGREDIENTS

1 garlic clove, crushed (minced)
2.5 cm/1 inch piece root (fresh)
   ginger, finely chopped
1 fresh green chilli, deseeded and
   finely chopped
6 tbsp low-fat natural (unsweetened)
   yogurt
1 tbsp tomato purée (paste)

1 tsp ground turmeric
1 tsp garam masala
1 tbsp lime juice
4 boneless, skinless chicken breasts,
   each 125 g/4$^{1}/_2$ oz
salt and pepper
wedges of lime or lemon, to serve

RELISH:
4 medium tomatoes
$^{1}/_4$ cucumber
1 small red onion
2 tbsp fresh coriander (cilantro),
   chopped

1 Preheat the oven to 190°C/
375°F/Gas Mark 5. In a small
bowl mix together the garlic,
ginger, chilli, yogurt, tomato
purée (paste), turmeric, garam
masala, lime juice and seasoning.

2 Wash and pat dry the chicken
breasts and place them on a
baking sheet. Brush or spread the
spicy yogurt mix over the chicken
and bake in the oven for 30–35

minutes until the meat is tender
and cooked through.

3 Meanwhile, make the relish.
Finely chop the tomatoes,
cucumber and onion and mix
together with the coriander
(cilantro). Season, cover and chill
until required.

4 Drain the cooked chicken on
absorbent kitchen paper and

serve hot with the relish. Or, allow
to cool, chill for at least 1 hour and
serve sliced as part of a salad.

VARIATION

The spicy yogurt coating would
work just as well if spread on a
chunky white fish such as cod fillet.
The cooking time should be reduced
to 15–20 minutes.

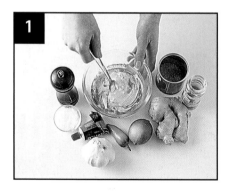

Grilled Chicken with Lemon & Honey

A good dish for the barbecue, this sweet and citrusy chicken can be served hot or cold. Sesame-flavoured noodles are the ideal accompaniment for the hot version.

Serves 4

CALORIES PER SERVING: 403 • FAT CONTENT PER SERVING: 4.7 G

INGREDIENTS

4 boneless chicken breasts, about
   125 g/4¹/2 oz each
2 tbsp clear honey
1 tbsp dark soy sauce
1 tsp lemon rind, finely grated
1 tbsp lemon juice

salt and pepper

TO GARNISH:
1 tbsp fresh chives, chopped
lemon rind, finely grated

NOODLES:
225 g/8 oz rice noodles
2 tsp sesame oil
1 tbsp sesame seeds
1 tsp lemon rind, finely grated

1 Preheat the grill (broiler) to medium. Skin and trim the chicken breasts to remove any excess fat, then wash and pat them dry with absorbent kitchen paper. Using a sharp knife, score the chicken breasts with a criss-cross pattern on both sides (making sure that you do not cut all the way through the meat).

2 Mix together the honey, soy sauce, lemon rind and juice in a small bowl, and then season well with black pepper.

3 Arrange the chicken breasts on the grill (broiler) rack and brush with half the honey mixture. Cook for 10 minutes, turn over and brush with the remaining mixture. Cook for a further 8–10 minutes or until cooked through.

4 Meanwhile, prepare the noodles according to the instructions on the packet. Drain well and pile into a warm serving bowl. Mix the noodles with the sesame oil, sesame seeds and the lemon rind. Season and keep warm.

5 Drain the chicken and serve with a small mound of noodles, garnished with chopped chives and lemon zest.

VARIATION

For a different flavour, replace the lemon with orange or lime. If you prefer, serve the chicken with boiled rice or pasta, which you can flavour with sesame seeds and citrus rind in the same way.

Chicken & Plum Casserole

Full of the flavours of autumn (fall), this combination of lean chicken, shallots, garlic and fresh, juicy plums is a very fruity blend. Serve with bread to mop up the gravy.

Serves 4

CALORIES PER SERVING: 285 • FAT CONTENT PER SERVING: 6.4 G

INGREDIENTS

2 rashers lean back bacon, rinds removed, trimmed and chopped
1 tbsp sunflower oil
450 g/1 lb skinless, boneless chicken thighs, cut into 4 equal strips
1 garlic clove, crushed
175 g/6 oz shallots, halved

225 g/8 oz plums, halved or quartered (if large) and stoned
1 tbsp light muscovado sugar
150 ml/5 fl oz/²/₃ cup dry sherry
2 tbsp plum sauce
450 ml/16 fl oz/2 cups fresh chicken stock

2 tsp cornflour (cornstarch) mixed with 4 tsp cold water
2 tbsp fresh parsley, chopped, to garnish
crusty bread, to serve

1 In a large, non-stick frying pan (skillet), dry fry the bacon for 2–3 minutes until the juices run out. Remove the bacon from the pan with a slotted spoon, set aside and keep warm.

2 In the same frying pan (skillet), heat the oil and fry the chicken with the garlic and shallots for 4–5 minutes, stirring occasionally, until well browned all over.

3 Return the bacon to the pan and stir in the plums, sugar, sherry, plum sauce and stock. Bring to the boil and simmer for 20 minutes until the plums have softened and the chicken is cooked through.

4 Add the cornflour (cornstarch) mixture to the pan and cook, stirring, for a further 2–3 minutes until thickened.

5 Spoon the casserole on to warm serving plates and garnish with chopped parsley. Serve with chunks of bread to mop up the fruity gravy.

VARIATION

Chunks of lean turkey or pork would also go well with this combination of flavours. The cooking time will remain the same.

Orange Turkey with Rice & Green Vegetables

This is a good way to use up left-over rice. You could use fresh or canned sweet pink grapefruit for an interesting alternative.

Serves 4

CALORIES PER SERVING: 354 • FAT CONTENT PER SERVING: 5.5 G

INGREDIENTS

1 tbsp olive oil
1 medium onion, chopped
450 g/1 lb skinless lean turkey (such as fillet), cut into thin strips
300 ml/^{1}/$_2$ pint/1^1/$_4$ cups unsweetened orange juice

1 bay leaf
225 g/8 oz small broccoli florets
1 large courgette (zucchini), diced
1 large orange
350 g/12 oz/6 cups cooked brown rice
salt and pepper

tomato and onion, to serve

TO GARNISH:
25 g/1 oz pitted black olives in brine, drained and quartered
bunch fresh basil leaves

1 Heat the oil in a large frying pan (skillet) and fry the onion and turkey, stirring, for 4–5 minutes until lightly browned.

2 Pour in the orange juice and add the bay leaf and seasoning. Bring to the boil and simmer for 10 minutes.

3 Meanwhile, bring a large saucepan of water to the boil and cook the broccoli florets, covered, for 2 minutes. Add the diced courgette (zucchini), bring back to the boil, cover and cook for a further 3 minutes (do not overcook). Drain and set aside.

4 Using a sharp knife, peel off the skin and white pith from the orange. Slice down the orange to make thin, round slices, then cut each slice in half.

5 Stir the broccoli, courgette (zucchini), rice and orange slices into the turkey mixture. Gently mix together and heat through for a further 3–4 minutes until piping hot.

6 Transfer the turkey rice to warm serving plates and garnish with black olives and shredded basil leaves. Serve with a fresh tomato and onion salad.

Curried Turkey with Apricots & Sultanas

An easy-to-prepare supper dish of lean turkey in a fruit curry sauce served on a bed of spicy rice.

Serves 4

CALORIES PER SERVING: 418 • FAT CONTENT PER SERVING: 7.9 G

INGREDIENTS

1 tbsp vegetable oil
1 large onion, chopped
450 g/1 lb skinless turkey breast, cut into 2.5 cm/1 inch cubes
3 tbsp mild curry paste
300 ml/$^1/_2$ pint/$1^1/_4$ cups fresh chicken stock

175 g/6 oz frozen peas
410 g/14$^1/_2$ oz can apricot halves in natural juice
50 g/1$^3/_4$ oz/$^1/_3$ cup sultanas
350 g/12 oz/6 cups Basmati rice, freshly cooked
1 tsp ground coriander

4 tbsp fresh coriander (cilantro), chopped
1 green chilli, deseeded and sliced
salt and pepper

1 Heat the oil in a large saucepan and gently fry the onion and turkey for 4–5 minutes until the onion has softened and the turkey is a light golden colour.

2 Stir in the curry paste. Pour in the stock, stirring, and bring to the boil. Cover and simmer for 15 minutes. Stir in the peas and bring back to the boil. Cover and simmer for 5 minutes.

3 Drain the apricots, reserving the juice, and cut into thick slices. Add to the curry, stirring in a little of the juice if the mixture is becoming dry. Add the sultanas and cook for 2 minutes.

4 Mix the rice with the ground and fresh coriander (cilantro), stir in the chilli and season well. Transfer the rice to warm plates and top with the curry.

VARIATION

Peaches can be used instead of the apricots if you prefer. Cook in exactly the same way.

Turkey Loaf with Courgettes (Zucchini) & Tomato

An easy-to-make dish that looks impressive. Lean turkey, flavoured with herbs and a layer of juicy tomatoes, is covered with courgette (zucchini) ribbons.

Serves 6

CALORIES PER SERVING: 179 • FAT CONTENT PER SERVING: 2.7 G

INGREDIENTS

1 medium onion, finely chopped
1 garlic clove, crushed
900 g/2 lb lean turkey, minced
  (ground)

1 tbsp fresh parsley, chopped
1 tbsp fresh chives, chopped
1 tbsp fresh tarragon, chopped
1 medium egg white, lightly beaten

1 medium, 1 large courgette (zucchini)
2 medium tomatoes
salt and pepper
tomato and herb sauce, to serve

1 Preheat the oven to 190°C/ 375°F/Gas Mark 5 and line a non-stick loaf tin with baking parchment. Place the onion, garlic and turkey in a bowl, add the herbs and season well. Mix together with your hands, then add the egg white to bind.

2 Press half of the turkey mixture into the base of the tin. Thinly slice the medium courgette (zucchini) and the tomatoes and arrange the slices over the meat. Top with the rest of the turkey and press down firmly.

3 Cover with a layer of kitchen foil and place in a roasting tin. Pour in enough boiling water to come half-way up the sides of the loaf tin. Bake in the oven for 1–1¼ hours, removing the foil for the last 20 minutes of cooking. Test the loaf is cooked by inserting a skewer into the centre – the juices should run clear. The loaf will also shrink away from the sides of the tin.

4 Meanwhile, trim the large courgette (zucchini). Using a vegetable peeler or hand-held metal cheese slicer, cut the courgette (zucchini) into thin ribbons. Bring a saucepan of water to the boil and blanch the ribbons for 1–2 minutes until just tender. Drain and keep warm.

5 Transfer the turkey loaf to a warm platter. Drape over the courgette (zucchini) ribbons and serve with a tomato and herb sauce.

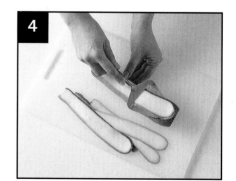

Duck with Kiwi Fruit & Raspberries

Duck is a rich meat and is best accompanied with fruit, as in this sophisticated dinner dish.

Serves 4

CALORIES PER SERVING: 286 • FAT CONTENT PER SERVING: 8.4 G

INGREDIENTS

450 g/1 lb boneless duck breasts,
   skin removed
2 tbsp raspberry vinegar
2 tbsp brandy
1 tbsp clear honey
1 tsp sunflower oil

salt and pepper

TO SERVE:
2 kiwi fruit, peeled and sliced thinly
assorted vegetables

SAUCE:
225 g/8 oz raspberries, thawed
   if frozen
300 ml/$\frac{1}{2}$ pint/$1\frac{1}{4}$ cups rosé wine
2 tsp cornflour (cornstarch) blended
   with 4 tsp cold water

1 Preheat the grill (broiler) to medium. Skin and trim the duck breasts to remove any excess fat. Using a sharp knife, score the flesh in diagonal lines and pound it with a meat mallet or a covered rolling pin until it is 1.5 cm/$\frac{3}{4}$ inch thick.

2 Place the duck breasts in a shallow dish. Mix together the vinegar, brandy and honey in a small bowl and pour it over the duck. Cover and leave to chill in the refrigerator for about 1 hour.

3 Drain the duck, reserving the marinade, and place on the grill (broiler) rack. Season and brush with a little oil. Cook for 10 minutes, turn over, season and brush with oil again, and cook for a further 8–10 minutes until the meat is cooked through.

4 Meanwhile, make the sauce. Reserving about 60 g/2 oz raspberries, place the rest in a pan. Add the reserved marinade and the wine. Bring to the boil and simmer for 5 minutes until slightly reduced.

5 Strain the sauce through a sieve, pressing the raspberries with the back of a spoon. Return the liquid to the saucepan and add the cornflour (cornstarch) paste. Heat through, stirring, until thickened. Add the reserved raspberries and season to taste.

6 Thinly slice the duck breast and arrange fanned out on warm serving plates, alternating with slices of kiwi fruit. Spoon over the sauce and serve with a selection of vegetables.

Roast Duck with Apples & Apricots

If you cannot buy portions of duckling, use a whole bird and cut it into joints. Always remove the skin before serving.

Serves 4

CALORIES PER SERVING: 313 • FAT CONTENT PER SERVING: 6.5 G

INGREDIENTS

4 duckling portions, 350 g/12 oz each
4 tbsp dark soy sauce
2 tbsp light muscovado sugar
2 red-skinned apples
2 green-skinned apples
juice of 1 lemon

2 tbsp clear honey
few bay leaves
salt and pepper
assorted fresh vegetables, to serve

SAUCE:
410 g/14^1/2 oz can apricots, in
   natural juice
4 tbsp sweet sherry

1 Preheat the oven to 190°C/375°F/Gas Mark 5. Wash the duck and trim away any excess fat. Place on a wire rack over a roasting pan and prick all over with a fork.

2 Brush the duck with the soy sauce. Sprinkle over the sugar and season with pepper. Cook in the oven, basting occasionally, for 50–60 minutes until the meat is cooked through – the juices should run clear when a skewer is inserted into the thickest part of the meat.

3 Meanwhile, core the apples and cut each into 6 wedges. Place in a bowl and mix with the lemon juice and honey. Transfer to a small roasting tin, add a few bay leaves and season. Cook alongside the duck, basting occasionally, for 20–25 minutes until tender. Discard the bay leaves.

4 To make the sauce, place the apricots in a blender or food processor together with the juice from the can and the sherry.

Process for a few seconds until smooth. Alternatively, mash the apricots with a fork until smooth and mix with the juice and sherry.

5 Just before serving, heat the apricot purée (paste) in a small pan. Remove the skin from the duck and pat the flesh with kitchen paper to absorb any fat.

6 Serve the duck with the apple wedges and the apricot sauce, and accompanied with vegetables.

Fish & Shellfish

Naturally low in fat yet rich in minerals and proteins, white fish and shellfish will be regular and important ingredients in any low-fat diet. There are so many flavours and textures available that the possible combinations are endless.

White fish, such as monkfish, haddock, cod and turbot, are widely available and easy to cook. Shellfish, too, are low in fat and rich in flavour, and they can be cooked in a variety of ways to produce mouthwatering, low-fat dishes. Some fishes – salmon, tuna, trout and mackerel, for example – are oily and should be eaten in moderation. They are rich in the fat-soluble vitamins A and D, however, and it is also believed that the oil in these fish is beneficial in breaking down cholesterol in the bloodstream.

Use this versatile ingredient in recipes that will soon become standards in your repertoire, from comforting Prawn and Tuna Pasta Bake and Fish Cakes with Piquant Tomato Sauce to sophisticated Five-spice Salmon with Ginger Stir Fry and Skewered Oriental Shellfish.

Prawn & Tuna Pasta Bake

This dish is ideal for a substantial supper. You can use whatever pasta you like, but the tricolour varieties will give the most colourful results.

Serves 4

CALORIES PER SERVING: 470 • FAT CONTENT PER SERVING: 8.5 G

INGREDIENTS

225 g/8 oz tricolour pasta shapes
1 tbsp vegetable oil
1 bunch spring onions (scallions), trimmed and chopped
175 g/6 oz button mushrooms, sliced
400 g/14 oz can tuna in brine, drained and flaked

175 g/6 oz peeled prawns (shrimp), thawed if frozen
2 tbsp cornflour (cornstarch)
425 ml/15 fl oz/1$\frac{3}{4}$ cups skimmed milk
4 medium tomatoes, sliced thinly
25 g/1 oz fresh breadcrumbs

25 g/1 oz reduced-fat Cheddar cheese, grated
salt and pepper

TO SERVE:
wholemeal bread
fresh salad

1 Preheat the oven to 190°C/ 375°F/Gas Mark 5. Bring a large saucepan of water to the boil and cook the pasta according to the instructions on the packet. Drain well.

2 Meanwhile, heat the oil in a frying pan (skillet) and fry all but a handful of the spring onions (scallions) and all of the mushrooms, stirring, for 4–5 minutes until softened.

3 Place the cooked pasta in a bowl and mix in the spring onions (scallions) and mushrooms, tuna and prawns (shrimp). Set aside until required.

4 Blend the cornflour (cornstarch) with a little milk to make a paste. Pour the remaining milk into a saucepan and stir in the paste. Heat, stirring, until the sauce begins to thicken. Season well.

5 Pour the sauce over the pasta mixture and stir until well combined. Transfer to the base of an ovenproof gratin dish and place on a baking sheet.

6 Arrange the tomato slices over the pasta and sprinkle with the breadcrumbs and cheese. Bake for 25–30 minutes until golden. Serve sprinkled with the reserved spring onions (scallions) and accompanied with bread and salad.

Fish Cakes with Piquant Tomato Sauce

*The combination of pink- and white-fleshed fish transforms
the humble fish cake into something a bit special.*

Serves 4

CALORIES PER SERVING: 320 • FAT CONTENT PER SERVING: 7.5 G

INGREDIENTS

450 g/1 lb potatoes, diced
225 g/8 oz haddock fillet
225 g/8 oz trout fillet
1 bay leaf
425 ml/15 fl oz/1^3/$_4$ cups fresh
 fish stock
2 tbsp low-fat natural fromage frais
 (unsweetened yogurt)

4 tbsp fresh snipped chives
75 g/2^3/$_4$ oz dry white breadcrumbs
1 tbsp sunflower oil
salt and pepper
fresh snipped chives, to garnish
lemon wedges, to serve

PIQUANT TOMATO SAUCE:
200 ml/7 fl oz/^{3}/$_4$ cup passata (sieved
 tomatoes)
4 tbsp dry white wine
4 tbsp low-fat natural (unsweetened)
 yogurt
chilli powder

1 Place the potatoes in a saucepan and cover with water. Bring to the boil and cook for 10 minutes or until tender. Drain well and mash.

2 Meanwhile, place the fish in a pan with the bay leaf and stock. Bring to the boil and simmer for 7–8 minutes until tender. Remove the fish with a slotted spoon and flake the flesh away from the skin.

3 Gently mix the cooked fish with the potato, fromage frais (unsweetened yogurt), chives and seasoning. Leave to cool, then cover and leave to chill for 1 hour.

4 Sprinkle the breadcrumbs on to a plate. Divide the fish mixture into 8 and form each portion into a patty, about 7.5 cm/ 3 inches in diameter. Press each fish cake into the breadcrumbs, coating all over.

5 Brush a frying pan (skillet) with oil and fry the fish cakes for 6 minutes. Turn the fish cakes over and cook for a further 5–6 minutes until golden. Drain on kitchen paper and keep warm.

6 To make the sauce, heat the passata (sieved tomatoes) and wine. Season, remove from the heat and stir in the yogurt. Return to the heat, sprinkle with chilli powder and serve with the fish cakes.

Provençale-style Mussels

These delicious large mussels are served hot with a tasty tomato and vegetable sauce.
If you can't find New Zealand mussels, serve the sauce with steamed fresh mussels.

Serves 4

CALORIES PER SERVING: 185 • FAT CONTENT PER SERVING: 6.5 G

INGREDIENTS

1 tbsp olive oil
1 large onion, finely chopped
1 garlic clove, finely chopped
1 small red (bell) pepper, deseeded
   and finely chopped
sprig of rosemary
2 bay leaves
400 g/14 oz can chopped tomatoes

150 ml/5 fl oz/$\frac{2}{3}$ cup white wine
1 courgette (zucchini), diced finely
2 tbsp tomato purée (paste)
1 tsp caster (superfine) sugar
50 g/1$\frac{3}{4}$ oz pitted black olives in
   brine, drained and chopped
675 g/1$\frac{1}{2}$ lb cooked New Zealand
   mussels in their shells

1 tsp orange rind
salt and pepper
crusty bread, to serve

TO GARNISH:
2 tbsp chopped, fresh parsley
orange slices

1   Heat the oil in a large saucepan and gently fry the onion, garlic and (bell) pepper for 3–4 minutes until just softened.

2   Add the sprig of rosemary and the bay leaves to the saucepan with the tomatoes and 100 ml/3$\frac{1}{2}$ fl oz/$\frac{1}{3}$ cup wine. Season with salt and pepper to taste, then bring to the boil and simmer for 15 minutes.

3   Stir in the courgette (zucchini), tomato purée (paste), sugar and olives. Simmer for 10 minutes.

4   Meanwhile, bring a pan of water to the boil. Arrange the mussels in a steamer or a large sieve (strainer) and place over the water. Sprinkle with the remaining wine and the orange rind. Cover and steam until the mussels open (discard any that remain closed).

5   Remove the mussels with a slotted spoon and arrange on a warm serving plate. Discard the herbs and spoon the sauce over the mussels. Garnish with chopped parsley and orange slices, and serve.

COOK'S TIP

Chop the vegetables for the sauce as finely as possible for best results.

Fish & Rice with Dark Rum

Based on a traditional Cuban recipe, this dish is similar to Spanish paella, but it has the added kick of dark rum. A meal in one, it needs only a simple salad accompaniment.

Serves 4

CALORIES PER SERVING: 575 • FAT CONTENT PER SERVING: 4.5 G

INGREDIENTS

450 g/1 lb firm white fish fillets (such as cod or monkfish), skinned and cut into 2.5 cm/1 inch cubes
2 tsp ground cumin
2 tsp dried oregano
2 tbsp lime juice
150 ml/5 fl oz/²⁄₃ cup dark rum
1 tbsp dark muscovado sugar

3 garlic cloves, chopped finely
1 large onion, chopped
1 medium red (bell) pepper, deseeded and sliced into rings
1 medium green (bell) pepper, deseeded and sliced into rings
1 medium yellow (bell) pepper, deseeded and sliced into rings

1.2 litres/2 pints/5 cups fish stock
350 g/12 oz/2 cups long-grain rice
salt and pepper
crusty bread, to serve

TO GARNISH:
fresh oregano leaves
lime wedges

1 Place the cubes of fish in a bowl and add the cumin, oregano, salt and pepper, lime juice, rum and sugar. Mix well, cover and leave to chill for 2 hours.

2 Meanwhile, place the garlic, onion and (bell) peppers in a large saucepan. Pour over the stock and stir in the rice. Bring to the boil, cover and leave to cook for 15 minutes.

3 Gently add the fish and the marinade juices to the pan. Bring back to the boil and simmer, uncovered, stirring occasionally but taking care not to break up the fish, for 10 minutes until the fish is cooked and the rice is tender.

4 Season to taste and transfer to a warm serving plate. Garnish with fresh oregano and lime wedges and serve with crusty bread.

VARIATION

If you prefer, use unsweetened orange juice in the marinade instead of the rum.

Seafood Stir Fry

This combination of assorted seafood and tender vegetables delicately flavoured with ginger makes an ideal light meal served with thread noodles.

Serves 4

CALORIES PER SERVING: 205 • FAT CONTENT PER SERVING: 6.5 G

INGREDIENTS

100 g/3½ oz small, thin asparagus spears, trimmed
1 tbsp sunflower oil
2.5 cm/1 inch piece root (fresh) ginger, cut into thin strips
1 medium leek, shredded
2 medium carrots, julienned

100 g/3½ oz baby sweetcorn, quartered lengthwise
2 tbsp light soy sauce
1 tbsp oyster sauce
1 tsp clear honey
450 g/1 lb cooked, assorted shellfish, thawed if frozen

freshly cooked egg noodles, to serve

TO GARNISH:
4 large cooked prawns
small bunch fresh chives

1 Bring a small saucepan of water to the boil and blanch the asparagus for 1–2 minutes. Drain the asparagus, set aside and keep warm.

2 Heat the oil in a wok or large frying pan (skillet) and stir-fry the ginger, leek, carrot and sweetcorn for about 3 minutes.

3 Add the soy sauce, oyster sauce and honey to the wok or frying pan (skillet). Stir in the shellfish and continue to stir-fry for 2–3 minutes until the vegetables are just tender and the shellfish are thoroughly heated through. Add the blanched asparagus and stir-fry for about 2 minutes.

4 To serve, pile the cooked noodles on to 4 warm serving plates and spoon over the seafood and vegetable stir fry. Serve garnished with a large prawn and freshly snipped chives.

COOK'S TIP

When you are preparing dense vegetables, such as carrots and other root vegetables, for stir frying, slice them into thin, evenly sized pieces so that they cook quickly and at the same rate. Delicate vegetables, such as (bell) peppers, leeks and spring onions (scallions), do not need to be cut as thinly.

Smoky Fish Pie

This flavoursome fish pie is perfect for a light supper.

Serves 4

CALORIES PER SERVING: 510 • FAT CONTENT PER SERVING: 6 G

INGREDIENTS

900 g/2 lb smoked haddock or
  cod fillets
600 ml/1 pint/2$\frac{1}{2}$ cups
  skimmed milk
2 bay leaves
115 g/4 oz button mushrooms,
  quartered

115 g/4 oz frozen peas
115 g/4 oz frozen sweetcorn kernels
675 g/1$\frac{1}{2}$ lb potatoes, diced
5 tbsp low-fat natural (unsweetened)
  yogurt
4 tbsp chopped fresh parsley

60 g/2 oz smoked salmon, sliced into
  thin strips
3 tbsp cornflour (cornstarch)
25 g/1 oz smoked cheese, grated
salt and pepper
wedges of lemon, to garnish

1 Preheat the oven to 200°C/
400°F/Gas Mark 6. Place the fish in a pan and add the milk and bay leaves. Bring to the boil, cover and then simmer for 5 minutes.

2 Add the mushrooms, peas and sweetcorn to the pan, bring back to a simmer, cover and cook for 5–7 minutes. Leave to cool.

3 Place the potatoes in a saucepan, cover with water, boil and cook for 8 minutes. Drain

well and mash with a fork or a potato masher. Stir in the yogurt, parsley and seasoning. Set aside.

4 Using a slotted spoon, remove the fish from the pan. Flake the cooked fish away from the skin and place in an ovenproof gratin dish. Reserve the cooking liquid.

5 Drain the vegetables, reserving the cooking liquid, and gently stir into the fish together with the salmon strips.

6 Blend a little cooking liquid into the cornflour (cornstarch) to make a paste. Transfer the rest of the liquid to a saucepan and add the paste. Heat through, stirring, until thickened. Discard the bay leaves and season to taste.

7 Pour the sauce over the fish and vegetables. Spoon over the mashed potato so that the fish is covered, sprinkle with cheese and bake for 25–30 minutes. Garnish with lemon wedges and serve.

Seafood Spaghetti

You can use whatever combination of shellfish you like in this recipe – it is poached in a savoury stock and served with freshly cooked spaghetti.

Serves 4

CALORIES PER SERVING: 400 • FAT CONTENT PER SERVING: 7 G

INGREDIENTS

2 tsp olive oil
1 small red onion, chopped finely
1 tbsp lemon juice
1 garlic clove, crushed
2 sticks celery, chopped finely
150 ml/5 fl oz/²/3 cup fresh fish stock

150 ml/5 fl oz/²/3 cup dry white wine
small bunch fresh tarragon
450 g/1 lb fresh mussels, prepared
225 g/8 oz fresh prawns (shrimp), peeled and deveined
225 g/8 oz baby squid, cleaned, trimmed and sliced into rings

8 small cooked crab claws, cracked and peeled
225 g/8 oz spaghetti
salt and pepper
2 tbsp chopped fresh tarragon, to garnish

1 Heat the oil in a large saucepan and fry the onion with the lemon juice, garlic and celery for 3–4 minutes until just softened.

2 Pour in the stock and wine. Bring to the boil and add the tarragon and mussels. Cover and simmer for 5 minutes. Add the prawns (shrimp), squid and crab claws to the pan, mix together and cook for 3–4 minutes until the mussels have opened, the prawns

(shrimp) are pink and the squid is opaque. Discard any mussels that have not opened and the tarragon.

3 Meanwhile, cook the spaghetti in a saucepan of boiling water according to the instructions on the packet. Drain well.

4 Add the spaghetti to the shellfish mixture and toss together. Season with salt and pepper to taste.

5 Transfer to warm serving plates and spoon over the cooking juices. Serve garnished with freshly chopped tarragon.

COOK'S TIP

Crab claws contain lean crab meat. Ask your fishmonger to crack the claws for you, leaving the pincers intact, because the shell is very tough.

Chilli- & Crab-stuffed Red Snapper

This popular fish is pinkish-red in colour and has moist, tender flesh.
For this recipe it is steamed, but it can also be baked or braised.

Serves 4

CALORIES PER SERVING: 120 • FAT CONTENT PER SERVING: 1 G

INGREDIENTS

4 red snappers, cleaned and scaled,
    about 175 g/6 oz each
2 tbsp dry sherry
salt and pepper
wedges of lime, to garnish

STUFFING:
1 small red chilli
1 garlic clove
1 spring onion (scallion)
1/2 tsp finely grated lime rind
1 tbsp lime juice

100 g/3 1/2 oz white crab meat, flaked

TO SERVE:
stir-fried shredded vegetables,
boiled white rice

1 Rinse the fish and pat dry on absorbent kitchen paper. Season inside and out and place in a shallow dish. Spoon over the sherry and set aside.

2 Meanwhile, make the stuffing. Carefully halve, deseed and finely chop the chilli. Place in a small bowl.

3 Peel and finely chop the garlic. Trim and finely chop the spring onion (scallion). Add to the chilli together with the grated lime rind, lime juice and the flaked crab meat. Season with salt and pepper to taste and combine. Press some of the stuffing into the cavity of each fish.

4 Bring a large saucepan of water to the boil. Arrange the fish in a steamer lined with baking parchment or in a large sieve (strainer) and place over the boiling water. Cover and steam for 10 minutes. Turn the fish over and steam for a further 10 minutes or until the fish is cooked.

5 Drain the fish and transfer to a serving plate. Garnish with wedges of lime and serve with stir-fried vegetables and white rice.

COOK'S TIP

Always wash your hands thoroughly after handling chillies as they can irritate your skin and eyes.

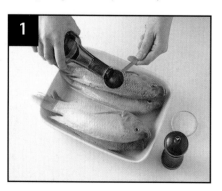

Citrus Fish Skewers

You can use your favourite fish for this dish as long as it is firm enough to thread on to a skewer. The tang of orange makes this a refreshing light meal.

Serves 4

CALORIES PER SERVING: 335 • FAT CONTENT PER SERVING: 14.5 G

INGREDIENTS

450 g/1 lb firm white fish fillets (such as cod or monkfish)
450 g/1 lb thick salmon fillet
2 large oranges
1 pink grapefruit

1 bunch fresh bay leaves
1 tsp finely grated lemon rind
3 tbsp lemon juice
2 tsp clear honey
2 garlic cloves, crushed

salt and pepper

TO SERVE:
crusty bread
mixed salad

1 Skin the white fish and the salmon, rinse and pat dry on absorbent kitchen paper. Cut each fillet into 16 pieces.

2 Using a sharp knife, remove the skin and pith from the oranges and grapefruit. Cut out the segments of flesh, removing all remaining traces of the pith and dividing membrane.

3 Thread the pieces of fish alternately with the orange and grapefruit segments and the bay leaves on to 8 skewers. Place the skewers in a shallow dish.

4 Mix together the lemon rind and juice, the honey and garlic. Pour over the fish skewers and season well. Cover and chill for 2 hours, turning occasionally.

5 Preheat the grill (broiler) to medium. Remove the skewers from the marinade and place on the rack. Cook for 7–8 minutes, turning once, until cooked through.

6 Drain, transfer to serving plates and serve with crusty bread and a fresh salad.

VARIATION

This dish makes an unusual starter. Try it with any firm fish – swordfish or shark, for example – or with tuna for a meatier texture.

Seafood Pizza

A change from the standard pizza toppings, this dish has piles of seafood baked with a red (bell) pepper and tomato sauce on a dill-flavoured bread base.

Serves 4

CALORIES PER SERVING: 315 • FAT CONTENT PER SERVING: 7 G

INGREDIENTS

145 g/5 oz standard pizza base mix
4 tbsp chopped fresh dill *or* 2 tbsp
  dried dill
fresh dill, to garnish

SAUCE:
1 large red (bell) pepper
400 g/14 oz can chopped tomatoes
  with onion and herbs

3 tbsp tomato purée (paste)
salt and pepper

TOPPING:
350 g/12 oz assorted cooked seafood,
  thawed if frozen
1 tbsp capers in brine, drained
25 g/1 oz pitted black olives in brine,
  drained

25 g/1 oz low-fat mozzarella cheese,
  grated
1 tbsp grated, fresh Parmesan cheese

1 Preheat the oven to 200°C/ 400°F/Gas Mark 6. Place the pizza base mix in a bowl and stir in the dill. Make the dough according to the instructions on the packet.

2 Press the dough into a round measuring 25.5 cm/10 inches across on a baking sheet lined with baking parchment. Set aside to prove (rise).

3 Preheat the grill (broiler) to hot. To make the sauce, halve and deseed the (bell) pepper and arrange on a grill (broiler) rack. Cook for 8–10 minutes until softened and charred. Leave to cool slightly, peel off the skin and chop the flesh.

4 Place the tomatoes and (bell) pepper in a saucepan. Bring to

the boil and simmer for 10 minutes. Stir in the tomato purée (paste) and season to taste.

5 Spread the sauce over the pizza base and top with the seafood. Sprinkle over the capers and olives, top with the cheeses and bake for 25–30 minutes. Garnish with sprigs of dill and serve hot.

Pan-seared Halibut with Red Onion Relish

Liven up firm steaks of white fish with a spicy, colourful relish. You can use white onions if you prefer, but red onions have a slightly sweeter flavour.

Serves 4

CALORIES PER SERVING: 250 • FAT CONTENT PER SERVING: 8 G

INGREDIENTS

1 tsp olive oil
4 halibut steaks, skinned, 175 g/6 oz
  each
$\frac{1}{2}$ tsp cornflour (cornstarch) mixed
  with 2 tsp cold water
salt and pepper

2 tbsp fresh chives, snipped,
  to garnish

RED ONION RELISH:
2 medium red onions
6 shallots

1 tbsp lemon juice
2 tsp olive oil
2 tbsp red wine vinegar
2 tsp caster (superfine) sugar
150 ml/5 fl oz/$\frac{2}{3}$ cup fresh fish stock

1 To make the relish, peel and thinly shred the onions and shallots. Place in a small bowl and toss in the lemon juice.

2 Heat 2 tsp oil in a pan and fry the onions and shallots for 3–4 minutes until just softened.

3 Add the vinegar and sugar and continue to cook for a further 2 minutes on a high heat.

Pour in the stock and season well. Bring to the boil and simmer gently for a further 8–9 minutes until the sauce has thickened and is slightly reduced.

4 Brush a non-stick, ridged frying pan (skillet) with oil and heat until hot. Press the steaks into the pan to seal, lower the heat and cook for 4 minutes. Turn the fish over and cook for 4–5 minutes

until cooked through. Drain on kitchen paper and keep warm.

5 Stir the cornflour (cornstarch) paste into the onion sauce and heat through, stirring, until thickened. Season to taste.

6 Pile the relish on to 4 warm serving plates and place a halibut steak on top of each. Garnish with chives and pepper.

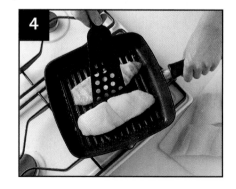

Five-spice Salmon with Ginger Stir Fry

Five-spice powder is a blend of star anise, fennel, cinnamon, cloves and Szechwan peppercorns (fagara) that is often used in Chinese dishes. It is a deliciously fragrant seasoning.

Serves 4

CALORIES PER SERVING: 295 • FAT CONTENT PER SERVING: 18 G

INGREDIENTS

4 salmon fillets, skinned, 115 g/4 oz each
2 tsp five-spice powder
pepper
1 large leek
1 large carrot

115 g/4 oz mangetout (snow peas)
2.5 cm/1 inch piece root (fresh) ginger
2 tbsp ginger wine
2 tbsp light soy sauce
1 tbsp vegetable oil

freshly boiled noodles, to serve

TO GARNISH:
leek, shredded
root (fresh) ginger, shredded
carrot, shredded

1 Wash the salmon and pat dry on absorbent kitchen paper. Rub the five-spice powder into both sides of the fish and season with freshly ground pepper. Set aside until required.

2 Trim the leek, slice it down the centre and rinse under cold water to remove any dirt. Finely shred the leek. Peel the carrot and cut it into very thin strips. Top and tail the mangetout (snow peas) and cut them into shreds. Peel the ginger and slice thinly into strips.

3 Place all of the vegetables into a large bowl and toss in the ginger wine and 1 tbsp soy sauce. Set aside.

4 Preheat the grill (broiler) to medium. Place the salmon fillets on the rack and brush with the remaining soy sauce. Cook for 2–3 minutes on each side until cooked through.

5 While the salmon is cooking, heat the oil in a non-stick wok or large frying pan (skillet) and stir-fry the vegetables for 5 minutes until just tender. Take care that you do not overcook the vegetables – they should still have bite. Transfer to serving plates.

6 Drain the salmon on kitchen paper and serve on a bed of stir-fried vegetables. Garnish with shredded leek, ginger and carrot and serve with noodles.

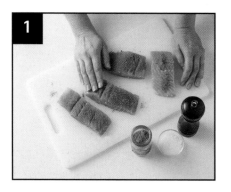

Skewered Oriental Shellfish

These shellfish and vegetable kebabs (kabobs) are ideal for serving at parties.
They are quick and easy to prepare and take next to no time to cook.

Makes 12

CALORIES PER SERVING: 100 • FAT CONTENT PER SERVING: 2.5 G

INGREDIENTS

350 g/12 oz raw tiger prawns
(shrimp), peeled leaving tails intact
350 g/12 oz scallops, cleaned,
trimmed and halved (quartered
if large)
1 bunch spring onions (scallions),
sliced into 2.5 cm/1 inch pieces
1 medium red (bell) pepper, deseeded
and cubed

100 g/3 1/2 oz baby corn, trimmed
and sliced into 1 cm/1/2 inch pieces
3 tbsp dark soy sauce
1/2 tsp hot chilli powder
1/2 tsp ground ginger
1 tbsp sunflower oil
1 red chilli, deseeded and sliced

DIP:
4 tbsp dark soy sauce
4 tbsp dry sherry
2 tsp clear honey
2.5 cm/1 inch piece root (fresh)
ginger, peeled and grated
1 spring onion (scallion), trimmed
and sliced very finely

1 Soak 12 wooden skewers in cold water for 10 minutes to prevent them from burning.

2 Divide the prawns (shrimp), scallops, spring onions (scallions), (bell) pepper and baby corn into 12 portions and thread on to the skewers. Cover the ends with foil so that they do not burn and place in a shallow dish.

3 Mix the soy sauce, chilli powder and ground ginger and coat the shellfish and vegetable kebabs (kabobs). Cover and leave to chill for about 2 hours.

4 Preheat the grill (broiler) to hot. Arrange the skewers on the rack, brush the shellfish and vegetables with oil and cook for 2–3 minutes on each side until the

prawns (shrimp) turn pink, the scallops become opaque and the vegetables are soft.

5 Mix together the dip ingredients and set aside.

6 Remove the foil and transfer the kebabs (kabobs) to a warm serving platter. Garnish with sliced chilli and serve with the dip.

Tuna Steaks with Fragrant Spices & Lime

Fresh tuna steaks are very meaty – they have a firm texture, yet the flesh is succulent. This recipe would be an impressive addition to a barbecue.

Serves 4

CALORIES PER SERVING: 200 • FAT CONTENT PER SERVING: 3.5 G

INGREDIENTS

4 tuna steaks, 175 g/6 oz each
1/2 tsp finely grated lime rind
1 garlic clove, crushed
2 tsp olive oil
1 tsp ground cumin

1 tsp ground coriander
pepper
1 tbsp lime juice
2 tbsp chopped fresh coriander
  (cilantro)

TO SERVE:
avocado relish (see Cook's Tip,
  below)
lime wedges

1 Trim the skin from the tuna steaks, rinse and pat dry on absorbent kitchen paper.

2 In a small bowl, mix together the lime rind, garlic, olive oil, cumin, coriander and pepper to make a paste.

3 Spread the paste thinly on both sides of the tuna. Heat a non-stick, ridged frying pan (skillet) until hot and press the tuna steaks into the pan to seal them. Lower the heat and cook for 5 minutes. Turn the fish over and cook for a further 4–5 minutes until the fish is cooked through. Drain on absorbent kitchen paper and transfer to a serving plate.

4 Sprinkle the lime juice and chopped coriander (cilantro) over the fish. Serve with freshly made avocado relish (see Cook's Tip, right) and lime wedges.

COOK'S TIP

For low-fat avocado relish to serve with tuna, peel and remove the stone from one small ripe avocado. Toss in 1 tbsp lime juice. Mix in 1 tbsp freshly chopped coriander (cilantro) and 1 small finely chopped red onion. Stir in some chopped fresh mango or a chopped medium tomato and season well.

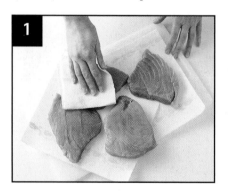

Baked Trout Mexican-style

You can make this dish as hot or as mild as you like by adding more or less red chilli to suit your taste. The green chillies are milder and add a refreshing pungency to the dish.

Serves 4

CALORIES PER SERVING: 235 • FAT CONTENT PER RECIPE: 5.5 G

INGREDIENTS

4 trout, 225 g/8 oz each
1 small bunch fresh coriander
  (cilantro)
4 shallots, shredded finely
1 small yellow (bell) pepper, deseeded
  and very finely chopped

1 small red (bell) pepper, deseeded
  and very finely chopped
2 green chillies, deseeded and
  finely chopped
1-2 red chillies, deseeded and
  finely chopped

1 tbsp lemon juice
1 tbsp white wine vinegar
2 tsp caster (superfine) sugar
salt and pepper
fresh coriander (cilantro), to garnish

1 Preheat the oven to 180°C/
350°F/Gas Mark 4. Wash the trout and pat dry with absorbent kitchen paper. Season the cavities and fill them with a few coriander (cilantro) leaves.

2 Place the fish side by side in a shallow ovenproof dish. Sprinkle over the shallots, (bell) peppers and chillies.

3 Mix together the lemon juice, vinegar and sugar in a bowl.

Spoon over the trout and season with salt and pepper. Cover the dish and bake for 30 minutes or until the fish is tender and the flesh is opaque.

4 Remove the the fish with a fish slice and drain. Transfer to warm serving plates and spoon the cooking juices over the fish. Garnish with fresh coriander (cilantro) and serve immediately with chilli bean rice, if you wish (see Cook's Tip, right).

COOK'S TIP

To make chilli bean rice to serve with this recipe, cook 225 g/8 oz/1¼ cup long-grain white rice in boiling water. Drain and return to the pan. Drain and rinse a 400 g/14 oz can kidney beans and stir into the rice along with 1 tsp each of ground cumin and ground coriander. Stir in 4 tbsp freshly chopped coriander (cilantro) and season well.

Vegetables & Salads

Too frequently, leaf vegetables are overcooked and limp, with all the goodness and flavour boiled out, while salads are often nothing more than a dismal leaf or two of pale green lettuce with a slice of tomato and a dry ring of onion. Make the most of the wonderful range of fresh produce that is available in our shops and markets.

Steam broccoli and cabbage so that they are colourful and crunchy. Enjoy the wonderfully appetizing shades of orange and yellow (bell) peppers and the almost unbelievable purple-brown of aubergine (eggplant). Trying grating root vegetables – carrots and daikon or mooli – to add flavour and texture to garnishes and casseroles. Look out for red and curly lettuces to bring excitement to an enticing summer salad. Use sweet baby tomatoes in salads and on skewers, and raid your garden and windowsill for sprigs of fresh mint and basil leaves.

Nuts and seeds are high in fat, so both should be used in moderation. However, they are a valuable source of protein and minerals, and vegetarians and vegans in particular need to ensure that their diets contain these valuable ingredients.

Vegetable Spaghetti with Lemon Dressing

Steaming vegetables helps to preserve their nutritional content and allow them to retain their bright, natural colours and crunchy texture.

Serves 4

CALORIES PER SERVING: 330 • FAT CONTENT PER SERVING: 2.5 G

INGREDIENTS

225 g/8 oz celeriac
2 medium carrots
2 medium leeks
1 small red (bell) pepper
1 small yellow (bell) pepper
2 garlic cloves
1 tsp celery seeds

1 tbsp lemon juice
300 g/10½ oz spaghetti
celery leaves, chopped, to garnish

LEMON DRESSING:
1 tsp finely grated lemon rind
1 tbsp lemon juice

4 tbsp low-fat natural fromage frais
(unsweetened yogurt)
salt and pepper
2 tbsp snipped fresh chives

1 Peel the celeriac and carrots, cut into thin matchsticks and place in a bowl. Trim and slice the leeks, rinse under running water to flush out any trapped dirt, then shred finely. Halve, deseed and slice the (bell) peppers. Peel and thinly slice the garlic. Add all of the vegetables to the bowl with the celeriac and the carrots.

2 Toss the vegetables with the celery seeds and lemon juice.

3 Bring a large saucepan of water to the boil and cook the spaghetti according to the instructions on the packet. Drain and keep warm.

4 Meanwhile, bring another large saucepan of water to the boil, put the vegetables in a steamer or sieve (strainer) and place over the boiling water. Cover and steam for 6–7 minutes or until just tender.

5 When the spaghetti and vegetables are cooked, mix the ingredients for the lemon dressing together.

6 Transfer the spaghetti and vegetables into a warm serving bowl and mix with the dressing. Garnish with chopped celery leaves and serve.

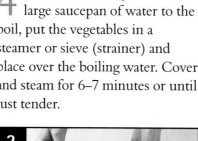

Pesto Pasta

Italian pesto is usually laden with fat. This version has just as much flavour but is much healthier.

Serves 4

CALORIES PER SERVING: 350 • FAT CONTENT PER SERVING: 4.5 G

INGREDIENTS

225 g/8 oz chestnut mushrooms,
  sliced
150 ml/5 fl oz/^{3}/4 cup fresh
  vegetable stock
175 g/6 oz asparagus, trimmed and
  cut into 5 cm/2 inch lengths
300 g/10^1/2 oz green and white
  tagliatelle

400 g/14 oz canned artichoke hearts,
  drained and halved
Grissini (bread sticks), to serve

TO GARNISH:
basil leaves, shredded
Parmesan shavings

PESTO:
2 large garlic cloves, crushed
15 g/^{1}/2 oz fresh basil leaves, washed
6 tbsp low-fat natural fromage frais
  (unsweetened yogurt)
2 tbsp freshly grated Parmesan
  cheese
salt and pepper

1 Place the sliced mushrooms in a saucepan along with the stock. Bring to the boil, cover and simmer for 3–4 minutes until just tender. Drain and set aside, reserving the liquor to use in soups if wished.

2 Bring a small saucepan of water to the boil and cook the asparagus for 3–4 minutes until just tender. Drain and set aside until required.

3 Bring a large pan of lightly salted water to the boil and cook the tagliatelle according to the instructions on the packet. Drain, return to the pan and keep warm.

4 Meanwhile, make the pesto. Place all of the ingredients in a blender or food processor and process for a few seconds until smooth. Alternatively, finely chop the basil and mix all the ingredients together.

5 Add the mushrooms, asparagus and artichoke hearts to the pasta and cook, stirring, over a low heat for 2–3 minutes. Remove from the heat, mix with the pesto and transfer to a warm bowl. Garnish with shredded basil leaves and Parmesan shavings and serve with Grissini (bread sticks).

Rice-stuffed Mushrooms

Flat mushrooms have a firm texture, which makes them ideal for baking. They are filled with the tender but more strongly flavoured wild mushrooms, although you can use ordinary varieties.

Serves 4

CALORIES PER SERVING: 315 • FAT CONTENT PER SERVING: 6 G

INGREDIENTS

4 large flat mushrooms
100 g/3^1/2 oz assorted wild
  mushrooms
4 dry-pack, sun-dried tomatoes,
  shredded
150 ml/5 fl oz/^{2}/3 cup dry red wine

4 spring onions (scallions), trimmed
  and finely chopped
75 g/2^3/4 oz/1^1/2 cups cooked
  red rice
salt and pepper
2 tbsp freshly grated Parmesan
  cheese

4 thick slices granary bread
spring onion (scallion), shredded,
  to garnish

1 Preheat the oven to 190°C/ 375°F/Gas Mark 5. Peel the flat mushrooms, pull out the stalks and set aside. Finely chop the stalks and place in a saucepan.

2 Add the wild mushrooms to the saucepan along with the tomatoes and red wine. Bring to the boil, cover and simmer gently for 2–3 minutes until just tender. Drain, reserving the cooking liquid, and place in a small bowl.

3 Gently stir in the chopped spring onions (scallions) and cooked rice. Season well and stuff into the flat mushrooms, pressing the mixture down gently. Sprinkle with the grated Parmesan cheese.

4 Arrange the mushrooms in an ovenproof baking dish and pour the reserved cooking juices around them. Bake in the oven for 20–25 minutes until they are just cooked.

5 Meanwhile, preheat the grill (broiler) to hot. Trim the crusts from the bread and toast on each side until lightly browned.

6 Drain the mushrooms and place each one on to a piece of toasted bread. Garnish with spring onions (scallions) and serve.

Biryani with Caramelized Onions

An assortment of vegetables cooked with tender rice, flavoured and coloured with bright yellow turmeric and other warming Indian spices, is served with a topping of sweet caramelized onions.

Serves 4

CALORIES PER SERVING: 365 • FAT CONTENT PER SERVING: 4.5 G

INGREDIENTS

175 g/6 oz/1 cup Basmati rice, rinsed
60 g/2 oz/¹/₃ cup red lentils, rinsed
1 bay leaf
6 cardamom pods, split
1 tsp ground turmeric
6 cloves
1 tsp cumin seeds
1 cinnamon stick, broken

1 onion, chopped
225 g/8 oz cauliflower, broken into
   small florets
1 large carrot, diced
100 g/3¹/₂ oz frozen peas
60 g/2 oz sultanas
600 ml/1 pint/2¹/₂ cups fresh
   vegetable stock
salt and pepper

2 tbsp chopped fresh coriander
   (cilantro), to garnish
naan bread, to serve

CARAMELIZED ONIONS:
2 tsp vegetable oil
1 medium red onion, shredded
1 medium onion, shredded
2 tsp caster (superfine) sugar

1 Place the rice, lentils, bay leaf, spices, onion, cauliflower, carrot, peas and sultanas in a large saucepan. Season with salt and pepper and mix well.

2 Pour in the stock, bring to the boil, cover and simmer for 15 minutes, stirring occasionally, until the rice is tender. Remove from the heat and leave to stand, covered, for 10 minutes to allow the stock to be absorbed. Discard the bay leaf, cardamom pods, cloves and cinnamon stick.

3 Meanwhile, make the caramelized onions. Heat the oil in a frying pan (skillet) and fry the onions over a medium heat for 3–4 minutes until just softened. Add the caster (superfine) sugar, raise the heat and cook, stirring, for a further 2–3 minutes until the onions are golden.

4 Gently mix the rice and vegetables and pile on to warm serving plates. Garnish with chopped coriander (cilantro), spoon over the caramelized onion and serve with plain, warmed naan bread.

Soft Pancakes with Stir-fried Vegetables & Tofu (Bean Curd)

Chinese pancakes are made without hardly any fat – they are simply flattened white flour dough.

Serves 4

CALORIES PER SERVING: 215 • FAT CONTENT PER SERVING: 8.5 G

INGREDIENTS

1 tbsp vegetable oil
1 garlic clove, crushed
2.5 cm/1 inch piece root (fresh)
   ginger, grated
1 bunch spring onions (scallions),
   trimmed and shredded lengthwise
100 g/3$^1/_2$ oz mangetout (snow
   peas), topped, tailed and shredded
225 g/8 oz tofu (bean curd), drained
   and cut into 1 cm/$^1/_2$ inch pieces

2 tbsp dark soy sauce, plus extra
   to serve
2 tbsp Hoisin sauce, plus extra
   to serve
60 g/2 oz canned bamboo shoots,
   drained
60 g/2 oz canned water chestnuts,
   drained and sliced
100 g/3$^1/_2$ oz beansprouts

1 small red chilli, deseeded and
   sliced thinly
1 small bunch fresh chives
12 soft Chinese pancakes

TO SERVE:
shredded Chinese leaves
1 cucumber, sliced
strips of red chilli

1 Heat the oil in a non-stick wok or a large frying pan (skillet) and stir-fry the garlic and ginger for 1 minute.

2 Add the spring onions (scallions), mangetout (snow peas), tofu (bean curd), soy and Hoisin sauces. Stir-fry for 2 minutes.

3 Add the bamboo shoots, water chestnuts, beansprouts and sliced red chilli to the pan. Stir-fry gently for a further 2 minutes until the vegetables are just tender but still have bite. Snip the chives into 2.5 cm/1 inch lengths and stir them into the mixture in the pan.

4 Meanwhile, heat the pancakes according to the instructions on the packet and keep warm.

5 Divide the vegetables and tofu (bean curd) among the pancakes. Roll up the pancakes, and serve with the Chinese leaves and extra sauce for dipping.

Char-grilled Mediterranean Vegetable Skewers

This medley of (bell) peppers, courgettes (zucchini), aubergine (eggplant) and red onion can be served on its own or as an unusual side dish.

Makes 8

CALORIES PER SERVING: 65 • FAT CONTENT PER SERVING: 2.5 G

INGREDIENTS

1 large red (bell) pepper
1 large green (bell) pepper
1 large orange (bell) pepper
1 large courgette (zucchini)
4 baby aubergines (eggplant)
2 medium red onions

2 tbsp lemon juice
1 tbsp olive oil
1 garlic clove, crushed
1 tbsp chopped, fresh rosemary *or*
  1 tsp dried rosemary
salt and pepper

TO SERVE:
cracked wheat
tomato and olive relish

1 Halve and deseed the (bell) peppers and cut into even sized pieces, about 2.5 cm/1 inch wide. Trim the courgettes (zucchini), cut in half lengthwise and slice into 2.5 cm/1 inch pieces. Place the (bell) peppers and courgettes (zucchini) into a large bowl and set aside.

2 Trim the aubergines (eggplant) and quarter them lengthwise. Peel the onions, then cut each one into 8 even-sized wedges. Add the aubergines and onions to the bowl containing the (bell) peppers and courgettes (zucchini).

3 In a small bowl, mix together the lemon juice, olive oil, garlic, rosemary and seasoning. Pour the mixture over the vegetables and stir to coat.

4 Preheat the grill (broiler) to medium. Thread the vegetables on to 8 skewers. Arrange the skewers on the rack and cook for 10–12 minutes, turning frequently until the vegetables are lightly charred and just softened.

5 Drain the vegetable skewers and serve on a bed of cracked wheat accompanied with a tomato and olive relish, if wished.

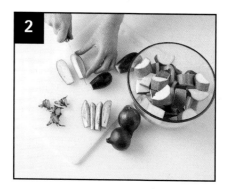

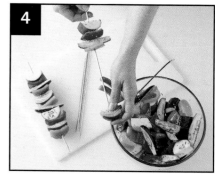

Stuffed Vegetables Middle Eastern-style

You can fill your favourite vegetables with this nutty tasting combination of cracked wheat, tomatoes and cucumber, with the flavours of cumin, coriander (cilantro) and mint.

Serves 4

CALORIES PER SERVING: 330 • FAT CONTENT PER SERVING: 5.5 G

INGREDIENTS

4 large beefsteak tomatoes
4 medium courgettes (zucchini)
2 orange (bell) peppers
salt and pepper

TO SERVE:
warm pitta bread and low-fat hummus

FILLING:
225 g/8 oz/1¼ cups cracked wheat
¼ cucumber
1 medium red onion
2 tbsp lemon juice
2 tbsp chopped fresh coriander
   (cilantro)

2 tbsp chopped fresh mint
1 tbsp olive oil
2 tsp cumin seeds

1 Preheat the oven to 200°C/ 400°F/Gas Mark 6. Cut off the tops from the tomatoes and reserve. Using a teaspoon, scoop out the tomato pulp, chop and place in a bowl. Season the tomato shells, then turn them upside down on absorbent kitchen paper.

2 Trim the courgettes (zucchini) and cut a V-shaped groove lengthwise down each one. Finely chop the cut-out courgette (zucchini) and add to the tomato

pulp. Season the courgettes (zucchini) shells and set aside.

3 Halve the (bell) peppers. Leaving the stalks intact, cut out the seeds and discard. Season the (bell) pepper shells and set aside.

4 To make the filling, soak the cracked wheat according to the instructions on the packet. Finely chop the cucumber and add to the reserved tomato pulp and courgette (zucchini) mixture.

5 Finely chop the onion, and add to the vegetable mixture with the lemon juice, herbs, olive oil, cumin and seasoning and mix together well.

6 When the wheat has soaked, mix with the vegetables and stuff into the tomato, courgette (zucchini) and (bell) pepper shells. Place the tops on the tomatoes, transfer to a roasting tin and bake for 20–25 minutes until cooked through. Drain and serve.

Fragrant Asparagus & Orange Risotto

Soft, creamy rice combines with the flavours of citrus and light aniseed to make this delicious supper for four or a substantial starter for six.

Serves 4–6

CALORIES PER SERVING: 420–280 • FAT CONTENT PER SERVING: 7.5–5 G

INGREDIENTS

115 g/4 oz fine asparagus
  spears, trimmed
1.2 litres/2 pints/5 cups
  vegetable stock
2 bulbs fennel

25 g/1 oz low-fat spread
1 tsp olive oil
2 sticks celery, trimmed and chopped
2 medium leeks, trimmed
  and shredded

350 g/12 oz/2 cups arborio rice
3 medium oranges
salt and pepper

1 Bring a small saucepan of water to the boil and cook the asparagus for 1 minute. Drain and set aside.

2 Pour the stock into a saucepan and bring to the boil. Reduce the heat to maintain a gentle simmer.

3 Meanwhile, trim the fennel, reserving the fronds, and cut into thin slices. Carefully melt the low-fat spread with the oil in a large saucepan, taking care that the water in the low-fat spread does not evaporate, and gently fry the fennel, celery and leeks for 3–4 minutes until just softened. Add the rice and cook, stirring, for a further 2 minutes until mixed.

4 Add a ladleful of stock to the pan and cook gently, stirring, until absorbed. Continue ladling the stock into the rice until the rice becomes creamy, thick and tender. This process will take about 25 minutes and shouldn't be hurried.

5 Finely grate the rind and extract the juice from 1 orange and mix in to the rice. Carefully remove the peel and pith from the remaining oranges. Holding the fruit over the saucepan, cut out the orange segments and add to the rice, along with any juice that falls.

6 Stir the orange into the rice along with the asparagus spears. Season with salt and pepper, garnish with the reserved fennel fronds, and serve.

Spicy Black Eye Beans

A hearty casserole of black eye beans in a rich, sweet tomato sauce flavoured with treacle (molasses) and mustard. It is ideal served with crusty bread to mop up the sauce.

Serves 4

CALORIES PER SERVING: 445 • FAT CONTENT PER SERVING: 6 G

INGREDIENTS

350 g/12 oz/2 cups black eye beans, soaked overnight in cold water
1 tbsp vegetable oil
2 medium onions, chopped
1 tbsp clear honey
2 tbsp treacle (molasses)
4 tbsp dark soy sauce
1 tsp dry mustard powder

4 tbsp tomato purée (paste)
450 ml/16 fl oz/2 cups fresh vegetable stock
1 bay leaf
1 sprig each of rosemary, thyme and sage
1 small orange
pepper

1 tbsp cornflour (cornstarch)
2 medium red (bell) peppers, deseeded and diced
2 tbsp chopped fresh parsley, to garnish
crusty bread, to serve

1 Preheat the oven to 150°C/300°F/Gas Mark 2. Rinse the beans and place in a saucepan. Cover with water, bring to the boil and boil rapidly for 10 minutes. Drain and place in an ovenproof casserole dish.

2 Meanwhile, heat the oil in a frying pan (skillet) and fry the onions for 5 minutes. Stir in the honey, treacle (molasses), soy sauce, mustard and tomato purée (paste). Pour in the stock, bring to the boil and pour over the beans.

3 Tie the bay leaf and herbs together with a clean piece of string and add to the pan containing the beans. Using a vegetable peeler, pare off 3 pieces of orange rind and mix into the beans, along with plenty of pepper. Cover and bake for 1 hour.

4 Extract the juice from the orange and blend with the cornflour (cornstarch) to form a paste. Stir into the beans along with the red (bell) peppers. Cover and cook for 1 hour, until the sauce is rich and thick and the beans are tender. Discard the herbs and orange rind.

5 Garnish with chopped parsley and serve with crusty bread.

Mexican-style Pizzas

Ready-made pizza bases are topped with a chilli-flavoured tomato sauce and topped with kidney beans, cheese and jalapeño chillies in this blend of American, Italian and Mexican cooking.

Serves 4

CALORIES PER SERVING: 585 • FAT CONTENT PER SERVING: 16 G

INGREDIENTS

4 x ready-made individual
  pizza bases
1 tbsp olive oil
200 g/7 oz can chopped tomatoes
  with garlic and herbs
2 tbsp tomato purée (paste)

200 g/7 oz can kidney beans, drained
  and rinsed
115 g/4 oz sweetcorn kernels, thawed
  if frozen
1–2 tsp chilli sauce
1 large red onion, shredded

100 g/3^{1}/2 oz reduced-fat Cheddar
  cheese, grated
1 large green chilli, sliced into rings
2 tbsp fresh coriander (cilantro),
  chopped
salt and pepper

1 Preheat the oven to 220°C/ 425°F/Gas Mark 7. Arrange the pizza bases on a baking sheet and brush them lightly with the oil.

2 In a bowl, mix together the chopped tomatoes, tomato purée (paste), kidney beans and sweetcorn, and add chilli sauce to taste. Season with salt and pepper.

3 Spread the tomato and kidney bean mixture evenly over each pizza base to cover. Top each pizza with shredded onion and sprinkle with some grated cheese and a few slices of green chilli to taste. Bake in the oven for about 20 minutes until the vegetables are tender, the cheese has melted and the base is crisp and golden.

4 Remove the pizzas from the baking sheet and transfer to serving plates. Sprinkle with chopped coriander (cilantro) and serve immediately.

COOK'S TIP

For a low-fat Mexican-style salad to serve with this pizza, arrange sliced tomatoes, fresh coriander (cilantro) leaves and a few slices of a small, ripe avocado. Sprinkle with fresh lime juice and coarse sea salt. Avocados have quite a high oil content, so eat in moderation.

Aubergine (Eggplant) Pasta Cake

This dish would make a stunning dinner party dish, yet it contains simple ingredients and is easy to make. The 'cake' would serve six as a main course or eight as a filling starter.

Serves 6–8

CALORIES PER SERVING: 290–215 • FAT CONTENT PER SERVING: 7–5 G

INGREDIENTS

1 medium aubergine (eggplant)
300 g/10^1/$_2$ oz tricolour pasta shapes
115 g/4 oz low-fat soft cheese with
  garlic and herbs

350ml/12 fl oz/1^1/$_3$ cups passata
  (sieved tomatoes)
4 tbsp grated Parmesan cheese
1^1/$_2$ tsp dried oregano

2 tbsp dry white breadcrumbs
salt and pepper

1 Preheat the oven to 190°C/ 375°F/Gas Mark 5. Grease and line a 20.5 cm/8 inch round spring-form cake tin.

2 Trim the aubergine (eggplant) and slice lengthwise into slices about 5 mm/¼ inch thick. Place in a bowl, sprinkle with salt, and set aside for 30 minutes to remove any bitter juices. Rinse well under cold running water and drain.

3 Bring a saucepan of water to the boil and blanch the aubergine (eggplant) slices for 1 minute. Drain and pat dry using absorbent kitchen paper. Set aside.

4 Cook the pasta shapes according to the instructions on the packet; for best results, the pasta should be slightly undercooked. Drain well and return to the saucepan. Add the soft cheese and allow it to melt over the pasta.

5 Stir in the passata (sieved tomatoes), Parmesan cheese, oregano and seasoning. Set aside.

6 Arrange the aubergine (eggplant) over the base and sides of the tin, overlapping the slices and making sure there are no gaps.

7 Pile the pasta mixture into the tin, packing down well, and sprinkle with the breadcrumbs. Bake for 20 minutes and leave to stand for 15 minutes.

8 Loosen the cake round the edge with a palette knife and release from the tin. Turn out aubergine-side uppermost and serve hot.

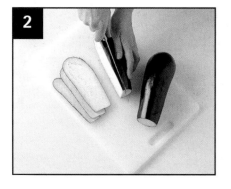

Mushroom Cannelloni

Thick pasta tubes are filled with a mixture of seasoned chopped mushrooms, and baked in a rich fragrant tomato sauce. Serve with shavings of Parmesan, if wished.

Serves 4

CALORIES PER SERVING: 315 • FAT CONTENT PER SERVING: 3.5 G

INGREDIENTS

350 g/12 oz chestnut mushrooms, chopped finely
1 medium onion, chopped finely
1 garlic clove, crushed
1 tbsp chopped fresh thyme
$^1/_2$ tsp ground nutmeg
4 tbsp dry white wine
4 tbsp fresh white breadcrumbs

12 dried 'quick-cook' cannelloni
salt and pepper
25 g/1 oz piece Parmesan cheese, to garnish (optional)

TOMATO SAUCE:
1 large red (bell) pepper
200 ml/7 fl oz/$^3/_4$ cup dry white wine
450 ml/16 fl oz/2 cups passata (sieved tomatoes)
2 tbsp tomato purée (paste)
2 bay leaves
1 tsp caster (superfine) sugar

1 Preheat the oven to 200°C/ 400°F/Gas Mark 6. Place the mushrooms, onion and garlic in a pan. Stir in the thyme, nutmeg and 4 tbsp wine. Bring to the boil, cover and simmer for 10 minutes.

2 Stir in the breadcrumbs to bind the mixture together and season. Cool for 10 minutes.

3 Preheat the grill (broiler) to hot. To make the sauce, halve and deseed the (bell) pepper, place on the grill (broiler) rack and cook for 8–10 minutes until charred. Leave to cool for 10 minutes.

4 Once the (bell) pepper has cooled, peel off the charred skin. Chop the flesh and place in a food processor with the wine. Blend until smooth, and pour into a pan.

5 Mix the remaining sauce ingredients with the (bell) pepper and wine and season. Bring to the boil and simmer for 10 minutes. Discard the bay leaves.

6 Cover the base of an ovenproof dish with a thin layer of sauce. Fill the cannelloni with the mushroom mixture and place in the dish. Spoon over the remaining sauce, cover with foil and bake for 35–40 minutes. Garnish with Parmesan (if using) and serve.

Tofu (Bean Curd) & Chickpea Burgers

Flavoured with spices, these burgers are delicious served with a tahini-flavoured relish.

Serves 4

CALORIES PER SERVING: 280 • FAT CONTENT PER SERVING: 9 G

INGREDIENTS

1 small red onion, chopped finely
1 garlic clove, crushed
1 tsp ground cumin
1 tsp ground coriander
2 tbsp lemon juice
425 g/15 oz can chickpeas (garbanzo beans), drained and rinsed
75 g/3 oz soft silken tofu (bean curd), drained
115 g/4 oz cooked potato, diced

4 tbsp freshly chopped coriander (cilantro)
2 tbsp plain (all-purpose) flour (optional)
75 g/2³/4 oz dry brown breadcrumbs
1 tbsp vegetable oil
burger buns
2 medium tomatoes, sliced
1 large carrot, grated
salt and pepper

RELISH:
1 tsp tahini paste
4 tbsp low-fat natural fromage frais (unsweetened yogurt)
2.5 cm/1 inch piece cucumber, finely chopped
1 tbsp chopped, fresh coriander (cilantro)
garlic salt, to season

1 Place the onion, garlic, spices and lemon juice in a pan, bring to the boil, cover and simmer for 5 minutes until softened.

2 Place the chickpeas (garbanzo beans), tofu (bean curd) and potato in a bowl and mash well. Stir in the onion mixture, coriander (cilantro) and seasoning, and mix together. Divide into 4 equal portions and form into patties 10 cm/4 inch across, dusting the hands with flour if necessary.

3 Sprinkle the breadcrumbs on to a plate and press the burgers into the crumbs to coat both sides.

4 Heat the oil in a large non-stick frying pan (skillet) and fry the burgers for 5 minutes on each side until heated through and golden. Drain on kitchen paper.

5 Meanwhile, mix all of the relish ingredients together in a bowl and leave to chill.

6 Line the buns with sliced tomato and grated carrot and top each with a burger. Serve with the relish spooned over.

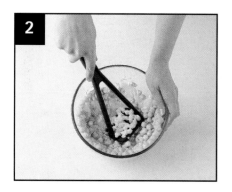

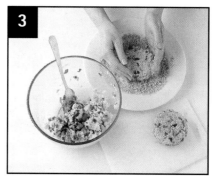

Sweet Potato & Leek Patties

Sweet potatoes have very dense flesh and a delicious, sweet, earthy taste.

Serves 4

CALORIES PER SERVING: 385 • FAT CONTENT PER SERVING: 6.5 G

INGREDIENTS

900 g/2 lb sweet potato
4 tsp sunflower oil
2 medium leeks, trimmed and finely
  chopped
1 garlic clove, crushed
2.5 cm/1 inch piece root (fresh)
  ginger, finely chopped
200 g/7 oz can sweetcorn kernels,
  drained

2 tbsp low-fat natural fromage frais
  (unsweetened yogurt)
60 g/2 oz wholemeal (whole wheat) flour
salt and pepper

GINGER SAUCE:
2 tbsp white wine vinegar
2 tsp caster (superfine) sugar
1 red chilli, deseeded and chopped

2.5 cm/1 inch piece root (fresh)
  ginger, cut into thin strips
2 tbsp ginger wine
4 tbsp fresh vegetable stock
1 tsp cornflour (cornstarch)

TO SERVE:
lettuce leaves
spring onions (scallions)

1 Peel the potatoes and cut into 2 cm/¾ inch thick pieces. Place in a saucepan, cover with water and boil for 10–15 minutes. Drain well and mash. Leave to cool.

2 Heat 2 tsp of oil and fry the leeks, garlic and chopped ginger for 2–3 minutes.

3 Stir the leek mixture into the potato with the sweetcorn, seasoning and fromage frais (unsweetened yogurt). Form into 8 patties and toss in flour to coat on both sides. Chill for 30 minutes.

4 Preheat the grill (broiler) to medium. Place the patties on a grill (broiler) rack and lightly brush with oil. Grill for 5 minutes, then turn over. Brush with oil and grill for a further 5 minutes, until golden. Drain on kitchen paper.

5 To make the sauce, place the vinegar, sugar, chilli and ginger in a pan. Bring to the boil and simmer for 5 minutes. Stir in the ginger wine. Blend the stock and cornflour (cornstarch) to form a paste and stir into the sauce. Heat through, stirring, until thickened.

6 Transfer the patties to serving plates, spoon over the sauce and serve.

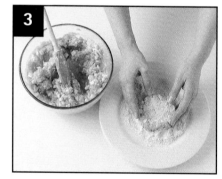

Ratatouille Vegetable Grill

Ratatouille is a French classic – a sumptuous dish of vegetables cooked in a tomato and herb sauce. Here it has a topping of diced potatoes and a golden layer of cheese.

Serves 4

CALORIES PER SERVING: 330 • FAT CONTENT PER SERVING: 4 G

INGREDIENTS

2 medium onions
1 garlic clove
1 medium red (bell) pepper
1 medium green (bell) pepper
1 medium aubergine (eggplant)

2 medium courgettes (zucchini)
2 x 400 g/14 oz cans chopped
   tomatoes
1 bouquet garni
2 tbsp tomato purée (paste)

900 g/2 lb potatoes
75 g/2³/₄ oz reduced-fat Cheddar
   cheese, grated
salt and pepper
2 tbsp snipped fresh chives, to garnish

1 Peel and finely chop the onions and garlic. Rinse, deseed and slice the (bell) peppers. Rinse, trim and cut the aubergine (eggplant) into small dice. Rinse, trim and thinly slice the courgettes (zucchini).

2 Place the onion, garlic and (bell) peppers into a large saucepan. Add the tomatoes, and stir in the bouquet garni, tomato purée (paste) and salt and pepper to taste. Bring to the boil, cover and simmer for 10 minutes, stirring half-way through.

3 Stir in the prepared aubergine (eggplant) and courgettes (zucchini) and cook, uncovered, for a further 10 minutes, stirring occasionally.

4 Meanwhile, peel the potatoes and cut into 2.5 cm/1 inch cubes. Place the potatoes into another saucepan and cover with water. Bring to the boil and cook for 10–12 minutes until tender. Drain and set aside.

5 Transfer the vegetables to a heatproof gratin dish. Pile the cooked potato cubes evenly over the vegetables.

6 Preheat the grill (broiler) to medium. Sprinkle grated cheese over the potatoes and place under the grill for 5 minutes until golden, bubbling and hot. Serve garnished with snipped chives.

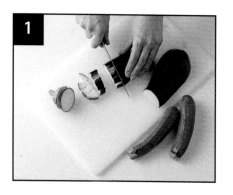

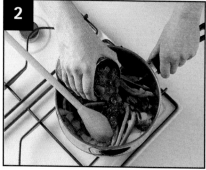

Mussel & Red (Bell) Pepper Salad

A colourful combination of cooked mussels tossed together with char-grilled red (bell) peppers, radicchio and rocket (arugula), and a lemon and chive dressing. It makes a delicious main meal.

Serves 4

CALORIES PER SERVING: 175 • FAT CONTENT PER SERVING: 6 G

INGREDIENTS

2 large red (bell) peppers
350 g/12 oz cooked shelled mussels, thawed if frozen
1 head of radicchio
25 g/1 oz rocket (arugula) leaves
8 cooked New Zealand mussels in their shells

TO SERVE:
lemon wedges
crusty bread

DRESSING:
1 tbsp olive oil
1 tbsp lemon juice

1 tsp finely grated lemon rind
2 tsp clear honey
1 tsp French mustard
1 tbsp snipped fresh chives
salt and pepper

1 Preheat the grill (broiler) to hot. Halve and deseed the (bell) peppers and place them skin-side up on the rack. Cook for 8–10 minutes until the skin is charred and blistered and the flesh is soft. Leave to cool for 10 minutes, then peel off the skin.

2 Slice the (bell) pepper flesh into thin strips and place in a bowl. Gently mix in the shelled mussels and set aside.

3 To make the dressing, mix all of the ingredients until well blended. Mix into the (bell) pepper and mussel mixture until coated.

4 Remove the central core of the radicchio and shred the leaves. Place in a serving bowl with the rocket (arugula) leaves and toss together.

5 Pile the mussel mixture into the centre of the leaves and arrange the large mussels round the edge of the dish. Serve with lemon wedges and crusty bread.

VARIATION

Replace the shelled mussels with peeled prawns (shrimp) and the New Zealand mussels with large crevettes, if you prefer. Lime could be used instead of lemon for a different citrus flavour.

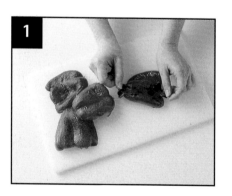

Sweet & Sour Fish Salad

This refreshing blend of pink and white fishes mixed with fresh pineapple and (bell) peppers would make an interesting starter or a light meal.

Serves 4

CALORIES PER SERVING: 190 • FAT CONTENT PER SERVING: 7 G

INGREDIENTS

225 g/8 oz trout fillets
225 g/8 oz white fish fillets (such as haddock or cod)
300 ml/¹/₂ pint/1¹/₄ cups water
1 stalk lemon grass
2 lime leaves
1 large red chilli
1 bunch spring onions (scallions), trimmed and shredded

115 g/4 oz fresh pineapple flesh, diced
1 small red (bell) pepper, deseeded and diced
1 bunch watercress, washed and trimmed
fresh snipped chives, to garnish

DRESSING:
1 tbsp sunflower oil
1 tbsp rice wine vinegar
pinch of chilli powder
1 tsp clear honey
salt and pepper

1 Rinse the fish, place in a frying pan (skillet) and pour over the water. Bend the lemon grass in half to bruise it and add to the pan with the lime leaves. Prick the chilli with a fork and add to the pan. Bring to the boil and simmer for 7–8 minutes. Let cool.

2 Drain the fish fillet, flake the flesh away from the skin and place in a bowl. Gently stir in the spring onions (scallions), pineapple and (bell) pepper.

3 Arrange the washed watercress on 4 serving plates, pile the cooked fish mixture on top and set aside.

4 To make the dressing, mix all the ingredients together and season well. Spoon over the fish and serve garnished with chives.

VARIATION

This recipe also works very well if you replace the fish with 350 g/12 oz white crab meat. Add a dash of Tabasco sauce if you like it hot!

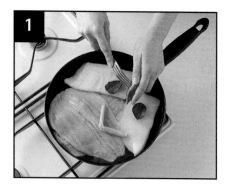

Beef & Peanut Salad

Although peanuts are very high in fat, they do have a strong flavour, so you can make a little go a long way. This recipe looks stunning if you arrange the ingredients rather than toss them together.

Serves 4

CALORIES PER SERVING: 320 • FAT CONTENT PER SERVING: 14 G

INGREDIENTS

$^1/_2$ head Chinese leaves
1 large carrot
115 g/4 oz radishes
100 g/$3^1/_2$ oz baby corn
1 tbsp ground nut oil
1 red chilli, deseeded and
  chopped finely

1 clove garlic, chopped finely
350 g/12 oz lean beef (such as fillet,
  sirloin or rump), trimmed and
  shredded finely
1 tbsp dark soy sauce
25 g/1 oz fresh peanuts (optional)
red chilli, sliced, to garnish

DRESSING:
1 tbsp smooth peanut butter
1 tsp caster (superfine) sugar
2 tbsp light soy sauce
1 tbsp sherry vinegar
salt and pepper

1 Finely shred the Chinese leaves and arrange on a platter. Peel the carrot and cut into thin, matchstick-like strips. Wash, trim and quarter the radishes, and halve the baby corn lengthwise. Arrange these ingredients around the edge of the dish and set aside.

2 Heat the oil in a non-stick wok or large frying pan (skillet) and stir-fry the chilli, garlic and beef for 5 minutes. Add the dark soy sauce and stir-fry for a further 1–2 minutes until tender and cooked through.

3 Meanwhile, make the dressing. Place all of the ingredients in a small bowl and blend them together until smooth.

4 Place the hot cooked beef in the centre of the salad ingredients. Spoon over the dressing and sprinkle with a few peanuts, if using. Garnish with slices of red chilli and serve immediately.

VARIATION

If preferred, use chicken, turkey, lean pork or even strips of venison instead of beef in this recipe. Cut off all visible fat before you begin.

Chicken & Spinach Salad

A simple combination of lean chicken with fresh young spinach leaves and a few fresh raspberries is served with a refreshing yogurt and honey dressing. This recipe is perfect for a summer lunch.

Serves 4

CALORIES PER SERVING: 225 • FAT CONTENT PER SERVING: 6 G

INGREDIENTS

4 boneless, skinless chicken breasts, 150 g/5¹/₂ oz each
450 ml/16 fl oz/2 cups fresh chicken stock
1 bay leaf
225 g/8 oz fresh young spinach leaves

1 small red onion, shredded
115 g/4 oz fresh raspberries
salt and freshly ground pink peppercorns
fresh toasted croûtons, to garnish

DRESSING:
4 tbsp low-fat natural (unsweetened) yogurt
1 tbsp raspberry vinegar
2 tsp clear honey

1 Place the chicken breasts in a frying pan (skillet). Pour over the stock and add the bay leaf. Bring to the boil, cover and simmer for 15–20 minutes, turning half-way through, until the chicken is cooked through. Allow to cool in the liquid.

2 Arrange the spinach on 4 serving plates and top with the onion. Cover and leave to chill.

3 Drain the cooked chicken and pat dry on absorbent kitchen paper. Slice the chicken breasts thinly and arrange, fanned out, over the spinach and onion. Sprinkle with the raspberries.

4 To make the dressing, mix all the ingredients together in a small bowl. Drizzle a spoonful of dressing over each chicken breast and season with salt and ground

pink peppercorns to taste. Serve with freshly toasted croûtons.

VARIATION

This recipe is delicious with smoked chicken, but it will be more expensive and richer, so use slightly less. It would make an impressive starter for a dinner party.

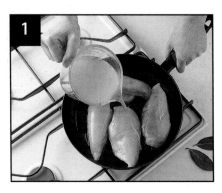

Pasta Provençale

A combination of Italian vegetables tossed in a tomato dressing, served on a bed of assorted salad leaves, makes a tasty main meal or an appetizing side dish.

Serves 4

CALORIES PER SERVING: 295 • FAT CONTENT PER SERVING: 6 G

INGREDIENTS

225 g/8 oz penne (quills)
1 tbsp olive oil
25 g/1 oz pitted black olives, drained and chopped
25 g/1 oz dry-pack sun-dried tomatoes, soaked, drained and chopped
100 g/3¹/₂ oz assorted baby salad leaves

400 g/14 oz can artichoke hearts, drained and halved
115 g/4 oz baby courgettes (zucchini), trimmed and sliced
115 g/4 oz baby plum tomatoes, halved
salt and pepper
shredded basil leaves, to garnish

DRESSING:
4 tbsp passata (sieved tomatoes)
2 tbsp low-fat natural fromage frais (unsweetened yogurt)
1 tbsp unsweetened orange juice
1 small bunch fresh basil, shredded

1 Cook the penne (quills) according to the instructions on the packet. Do not overcook the pasta – it should still have 'bite'. Drain well and return to the pan. Stir in the olive oil, salt and pepper, olives and sun-dried tomatoes. Leave to cool.

2 Gently mix the artichokes, courgettes (zucchini) and plum tomatoes into the cooked pasta. Arrange the salad leaves in a serving bowl.

3 To make the dressing, mix all the ingredients together and toss into the vegetables and pasta.

4 Spoon the mixture on top of the salad leaves and garnish with shredded basil leaves.

VARIATION

For a non-vegetarian version, stir 225 g/8 oz canned tuna in brine, drained and flaked, into the pasta together with the vegetables. Other pasta shapes can be included – look out for farfalle (bows) and rotelle (spoked wheels).

Root Vegetable Salad

This colourful salad of grated vegetables is perfect for a light starter.
The peppery flavours of the mooli and radishes are refreshingly pungent.
Serve with some toasted bread and assorted salad leaves.

Serves 4

CALORIES PER SERVING: 150 • FAT CONTENT PER SERVING: 9 G

INGREDIENTS

350 g/12 oz carrots
225 g/8 oz mooli (white radish)
115 g/4 oz radishes
350 g/12 oz celeriac
1 tbsp orange juice
2 sticks celery with leaves, washed
   and trimmed

100 g/3¹/₂ oz assorted salad leaves
25 g/1 oz walnut pieces

DRESSING:
1 tbsp walnut oil
1 tbsp white wine vinegar
1 tsp wholegrain mustard

¹/₂ tsp finely grated orange rind
1 tsp celery seeds
salt and pepper

1 Peel and coarsely grate or very finely shred the carrots, mooli (white radish) and radishes. Set aside in separate bowls.

2 Peel and coarsely grate or finely shred the celeriac and mix with the orange juice.

3 Remove the celery leaves and reserve. Finely chop the celery sticks.

4 Divide the salad leaves among 4 serving plates and arrange the vegetables in small piles on top. Set aside while you make the dressing.

5 Mix all of the dressing ingredients together and season well. Drizzle a little over each salad. Shred the reserved celery leaves and sprinkle over the salad with the walnut pieces.

COOK'S TIP

Also known as Chinese white radish and daikon, mooli resembles a large white parsnip. It has crisp, slightly pungent flesh, which can be eaten raw or cooked. It is a useful ingredient in stir-fries. Fresh mooli tend to have a stronger flavour than shop-bought ones.

Beetroot & Orange Rice Salad

You must use freshly cooked beetroot in this unusual combination of colours and flavours. Beetroot that has been soaked in vinegar will spoil the delicate balance.

Serves 4

CALORIES PER SERVING: 335 • FAT CONTENT PER SERVING: 2.5 G

INGREDIENTS

225 g/8 oz/1⅓ cups long-grain and
  wild rices (see Cook's Tip, below)
4 large oranges
450 g/1 lb cooked beetroot, peeled
2 heads of chicory
salt and pepper

fresh snipped chives, to garnish

DRESSING:
4 tbsp low-fat natural fromage frais
  (unsweetened yogurt)
1 garlic clove, crushed

1 tbsp wholegrain mustard
½ tsp finely grated orange rind
2 tsp clear honey

---

1 Cook the rices according to the instructions on the packet. Drain and set aside to cool.

2 Meanwhile, slice the top and bottom off each orange. Using a sharp knife, remove the skin and pith. Holding the orange over a bowl to catch the juice, carefully slice between each segment. Place the segments in a separate bowl. Cover the juice and leave to chill in the refrigerator until required.

3 Drain the beetroot if necessary and dice into cubes. Mix with the orange segments, cover and leave to chill.

4 When the rice has cooled, mix in the reserved orange juice and season with salt and pepper to taste.

5 Line 4 serving bowls or plates with the chicory leaves. Spoon over the rice and top with the beetroot and orange segments.

6 Mix all the dressing ingredients together and spoon over the salad, or serve separately in a bowl, if preferred. Garnish with fresh snipped chives.

COOK'S TIP

Look out for boxes of ready-mixed long-grain and wild rices. Alternatively, cook 175 g/6 oz/ 1 cup white rice and 60 g/2 oz/ ¼ cup wild rice separately.

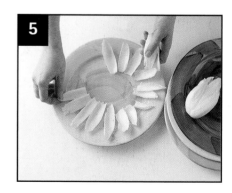

Red Hot Slaw

Red in colour and red-hot in taste, too – just how much chilli powder you add is up to you.
As well as being an exciting side dish, this salad makes a good filling for jacket potatoes.

Serves 4

CALORIES PER SERVING: 200 • FAT CONTENT PER SERVING: 8.5 G

INGREDIENTS

1/2 small red cabbage
1 large carrot
2 red-skinned apples
1 tbsp lemon juice
1 medium red onion
100 g/3 1/2 oz reduced-fat Cheddar
cheese, grated

TO GARNISH:
red chilli strips
carrot strips

DRESSING:
3 tbsp reduced-calorie mayonnaise
3 tbsp low-fat natural (unsweetened)
yogurt

1 garlic clove, crushed
1 tsp paprika
1–2 tsp chilli powder
pinch cayenne pepper (optional)
salt and pepper

1 Cut the red cabbage in half and remove the central core. Finely shred the leaves and place in a large bowl. Peel and coarsely grate or finely shred the carrot and mix into the cabbage.

2 Core the apples and finely dice, leaving on the skins. Place in another bowl and toss in the lemon juice to help prevent the apple from browning. Mix the apple into the cabbage and carrot.

3 Peel and finely shred or grate the onion. Stir into the other vegetables along with the cheese and mix together.

4 To make the dressing, mix together the mayonnaise, yogurt, garlic and paprika in a small bowl. Add chilli powder according to taste, and the cayenne pepper, if using – remember this will add more spice to the dressing. Season well.

5 Toss the dressing into the vegetables and mix well. Cover and leave to chill in the refrigerator for 1 hour to allow the flavours to develop. Serve garnished with strips of red chilli and carrot.

Pasta Niçoise Salad

Based on the classic French salad niçoise, this recipe contains pasta instead of potatoes. The very light olive oil dressing has the tang of capers and the fragrance of fresh basil.

Serves 4

CALORIES PER SERVING: 370 • FAT CONTENT PER SERVING: 9 G

INGREDIENTS

225 g/8 oz farfalle (bows)
175 g/6 oz French (green) beans, topped and tailed
350 g/12 oz fresh tuna steaks
115 g/4 oz baby plum tomatoes, halved
8 anchovy fillets, drained on absorbent kitchen paper

2 tbsp capers in brine, drained
25 g/1 oz pitted black olives in brine, drained
fresh basil leaves, to garnish
salt and pepper

DRESSING:
1 tbsp olive oil
1 garlic clove, crushed
1 tbsp lemon juice
1/2 tsp finely grated lemon rind
1 tbsp shredded fresh basil leaves

1 Cook the pasta in lightly salted boiling water according to the instructions on the packet until just cooked. Drain well, set aside and keep warm.

2 Bring a small saucepan of lightly salted water to the boil and cook the French (green) beans for 5–6 minutes until just tender. Drain well and toss into the pasta. Set aside and keep warm.

3 Preheat the grill (broiler) to medium. Rinse and pat the tuna steaks dry on absorbent kitchen paper. Season on both sides with black pepper. Place the tuna steaks on the grill (broiler) rack and cook for 4–5 minutes on each side until cooked through.

4 Drain the tuna on absorbent kitchen paper and flake into bite-sized pieces. Toss the tuna into the pasta along with the tomatoes, anchovies, capers and olives. Set aside and keep warm.

5 Meanwhile, prepare the dressing. Mix all the ingredients together and season well. Pour the dressing over the pasta mixture and mix carefully. Transfer to a warmed serving bowl and serve sprinkled with fresh basil leaves.

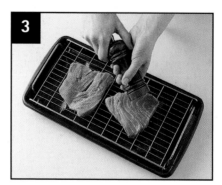

Coconut Couscous Salad

The nutty taste of toasted coconut really stands out in this delicious dish, which can also be served hot, without the dressing, to accompany a rich lamb stew.

Serves 4

CALORIES PER SERVING: 270 • FAT CONTENT PER SERVING: 10 G

INGREDIENTS

350 g/12 oz precooked couscous
175 g/6 oz no-need-to-soak
  dried apricots
1 small bunch fresh chives
2 tbsp unsweetened desiccated
  (shredded) coconut

1 tsp ground cinnamon
salt and pepper
mint leaves, to garnish

DRESSING:
1 tbsp olive oil

2 tbsp unsweetened orange juice
$\frac{1}{2}$ tsp finely grated orange rind
1 tsp wholegrain mustard
1 tsp clear honey
2 tbsp chopped fresh mint leaves

1 Soak the couscous according to the instructions on the packet. Bring a large saucepan of water to the boil. Transfer the couscous to a steamer or large sieve (strainer) lined with muslin (cheesecloth) and place over the water. Cover and steam as directed. Remove from the heat, place in heatproof bowl and set aside to cool.

2 Meanwhile, slice the apricots into thin strips and place in a small bowl. Using scissors, snip the chives over the apricots.

3 When the couscous is cool, mix in the apricots, chives, coconut and cinnamon. Season well.

4 To make the dressing, mix all the ingredients together and season. Pour over the couscous and mix until well combined. Cover and leave to chill for 1 hour to allow the flavours to develop. Serve garnished with mint leaves.

COOK'S TIP

To serve this salad hot, when the couscous has been steamed, mix in the apricots, chives, coconut, cinnamon and seasoning along with 1 tbsp olive oil. Pile into a warmed serving bowl and serve.

Baking & Desserts

The ideal ending to a meal is fresh fruit,
topped with low-fat yogurt or fromage frais. Fruit
contains no fat and is sweet enough to need extra sugar,
but it is a valuable source of vitamins and fibre – ideal
in every way for anyone who cares about their
own and their family's health.

There are, however, dozens of other ways
in which fruit can be used as the basis for desserts
and bakes, and thanks to modern transportation
systems the range of unusual and exotic fruits available
in supermarkets seems to expand every week.
Experiment with some of these unfamiliar fruits in
delicious warm desserts, sophisticated mousses
and fools, and satisfying cakes, and use old
favourites in enticing new ways.

From an elegant Strawberry Roulade to add
the perfect finishing touch to a dinner party to a
deliciously moist Carrot & Ginger Cake to offer to
unexpected guests, you will find the perfect recipe for
every occasion on the following pages.

Paper-thin Fruit Pies

The extra-crisp pastry cases, filled with slices of apple and pear and glazed with apricot jam, are best served hot with low-fat custard or low-fat fruit yogurt.

Serves 4

CALORIES PER SERVING: 185 • FAT CONTENT: 7.5 G

INGREDIENTS

1 medium eating (dessert) apple
1 medium ripe pear
2 tbsp lemon juice
60 g/2 oz low-fat spread

4 rectangular sheets of filo pastry,
  thawed if frozen
2 tbsp low-sugar apricot jam
1 tbsp unsweetened orange juice

1 tbsp finely chopped natural
  pistachio nuts, shelled
2 tsp icing (confectioner's) sugar,
  for dusting
low-fat custard, to serve

1 Preheat the oven to 200°C/ 400°F/Gas Mark 6. Core and thinly slice the apple and pear and toss them in the lemon juice.

2 Over a low heat, gently melt the low-fat spread.

3 Cut the sheets of pastry into 4 and cover with a clean, damp tea towel (dish cloth). Brush 4 non-stick Yorkshire pudding tins (large muffin pans), measuring 10 cm/4 inch across, with a little of the low-fat spread.

4 Working on each pie separately, brush 4 sheets of pastry with low-fat spread. Press a small sheet of pastry into the base of one tin. Arrange the other sheets of pastry on top at slightly different angles. Repeat with the other sheets of pastry to make another 3 pies.

5 Arrange the apple and pear slices alternately in the centre of each pastry case and lightly crimp the edges of the pastry of each pie.

6 Mix the jam and orange juice together until smooth and brush over the fruit. Bake for 12–15 minutes. Sprinkle over the nuts, dust lightly with icing (confectioner's) sugar and serve hot with low-fat custard.

VARIATION

Other combinations of fruit are equally delicious. Try peach and apricot, raspberry and apple, or pineapple and mango.

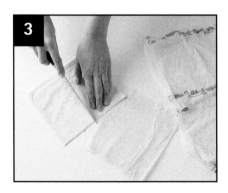

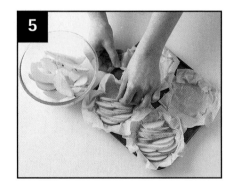

Almond Trifles

Amaretti biscuits can be made with ground almonds, which give them a high fat content. For this recipe, make sure you use the biscuits made from apricot kernels, which have a lower fat content.

Serves 4

CALORIES PER SERVING: 230 • FAT CONTENT PER SERVING: 3.5 G

INGREDIENTS

8 Amaretti di Saronno biscuits
4 tbsp brandy *or* Amaretti liqueur
225 g/8 oz raspberries, thawed
   if frozen

300 ml/^{1}/$_2$ pint/1^1/$_4$ cups
   low-fat custard
300 ml/^{1}/$_2$ pint/1^1/$_4$ cups low-fat
   natural fromage frais
   (unsweetened yogurt)

1 tsp almond essence (extract)
15 g/^{1}/$_2$ oz toasted almonds,
   flaked (slivered)
1 tsp cocoa powder

1 Place the biscuits in a mixing bowl and using a rolling pin, carefully crush the biscuits into small pieces.

2 Divide the crushed biscuits among 4 serving glasses. Sprinkle over the brandy or liqueur and leave to stand for about 30 minutes to allow the biscuits to soften.

3 Top the layer of biscuits with a layer of raspberries, reserving a few raspberries for decoration, and spoon over enough custard to just cover.

4 Mix the fromage frais (unsweetened yogurt) with the almond essence (extract) and spoon over the custard. Leave to chill in the refrigerator for about 30 minutes.

5 Just before serving, sprinkle over the toasted almonds and dust with cocoa powder. Decorate with the reserved raspberries and serve at once.

VARIATION

Try this trifle with assorted summer fruits. If they are a frozen mix, use them frozen and allow them to thaw so that the juices soak into the biscuit base – it will taste delicious.

Cheese Hearts with Strawberry Sauce

*These little moulds look very attractive when they are made in the French coeur
à la crème china moulds, but you could make them in small ramekins instead.*

Serves 4

CALORIES PER SERVING: 120 • FAT CONTENT PER SERVING: 0.6 G

INGREDIENTS

150 g/5$^{1}/_{2}$ oz low-fat cottage cheese
150 ml/5 fl oz/$^{2}/_{3}$ cup low-fat natural
   fromage frais (unsweetened yogurt)
1 medium egg white

2 tbsp caster (superfine) sugar
1–2 tsp vanilla essence (extract)
rose-scented geranium leaves,
   to decorate

SAUCE:
225 g/8 oz strawberries
4 tbsp unsweetened orange juice
2–3 tsp icing (confectioner's) sugar

1 Line 4 heart-shaped moulds with clean muslin (cheese-cloth). Place a sieve (strainer) over a mixing bowl and using the back of a metal spoon, press through the cottage cheese. Mix in the fromage frais (yogurt).

2 Whisk the egg white until stiff. Fold into the cheeses, with the caster (superfine) sugar and vanilla essence (extract).

3 Spoon the cheese mixture into the moulds and smooth over the tops. Place on a wire rack over a tray and leave to chill for 1 hour until firm and drained.

4 Meanwhile, make the sauce. Wash the strawberries under cold running water. Reserving a few strawberries for decoration, hull and chop the remainder. Place the strawberries in a blender or food processor with the orange juice and process until smooth. Alternatively, push through a sieve (strainer) to purée. Mix with the icing (confectioner's) sugar to taste. Cover and leave to chill until required.

5 Remove the cheese hearts from the moulds and transfer to serving plates. Remove the muslin (cheesecloth), decorate with strawberries and geranium leaves and serve with the sauce.

COOK'S TIP

The coeur à la crème moulds have drainage holes in them, so if you use ramekins or other small jelly moulds, the hearts will be much softer.

Almond & Sultana Cheesecakes

These creamy cheese desserts are so delicious that they are sure to become firm favourites – and it's hard to believe that they are low in fat.

Serves 4

CALORIES PER SERVING: 315 • FAT CONTENT PER SERVING: 16 G

INGREDIENTS

12 Amaretti di Saronno biscuits
1 medium egg white, lightly beaten
225 g/8 oz skimmed-milk soft cheese
1/2 tsp almond essence (extract)
1/2 tsp finely grated lime rind
25 g/1 oz ground almonds

25 g/1 oz caster (superfine) sugar
60 g/2 oz sultanas
2 tsp powdered gelatine
2 tbsp boiling water
2 tbsp lime juice

TO DECORATE:
25 g/1 oz flaked (slivered) toasted
   almonds
sliced lime

1 Preheat the oven to 180°C/ 350°F/Gas Mark 4. Place the biscuits in a clean plastic bag, seal the bag and using a rolling pin, crush them into small pieces. Place the crumbs in a bowl and bind together with the egg white.

2 Arrange 4 non-stick pastry rings or poached egg rings, 9 cm/3½ inches across, on a baking sheet lined with baking parchment. Divide the biscuit mixture into 4 equal portions and spoon it into the rings, pressing down well. Bake for 10 minutes until crisp and allow to cool in the rings.

3 Beat together the soft cheese, almond essence (extract), lime rind, ground almonds, sugar and sultanas until well mixed.

4 Dissolve the gelatine in the boiling water and stir in the lime juice. Fold into the cheese mixture and spoon over the biscuit bases. Smooth over the tops and chill for 1 hour or until set.

5 Loosen the cheesecakes from the tins using a small palette knife or spatula and transfer to serving plates. Decorate with flaked (slivered) toasted almonds and slices of fresh lime, and serve.

VARIATION

If you prefer, substitute chopped no-need-to-soak dried apricots for the sultanas.

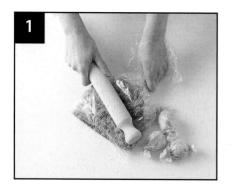

Red Fruits with Foaming Sauce

*A colourful combination of soft fruits, served with a frothy marshmallow
sauce, is an ideal dessert when summer fruits are in season.*

Serves 4

CALORIES PER SERVING: 220 • FAT CONTENT PER SERVING: 0.3 G

INGREDIENTS

225 g/8 oz redcurrants, washed and
trimmed, thawed if frozen
225 g/8 oz cranberries
75 g/3 oz light muscovado sugar

200 ml/7 fl oz/^{3}/$_4$ cup unsweetened
apple juice
1 cinnamon stick, broken
300 g/10^1/$_2$ oz small strawberries,
washed, hulled and halved

SAUCE:
225 g/8 oz raspberries, thawed
if frozen
2 tbsp fruit cordial
100 g/3^1/$_2$ oz marshmallows

1 Place the redcurrants,
cranberries and sugar in a
saucepan. Pour in the apple juice
and add the cinnamon stick. Bring
the mixture to the boil and
simmer gently for 10 minutes
until the fruit has just softened.

2 Stir the strawberries into the
cranberry and sugar mixture
and mix well. Transfer the mixture
to a bowl, cover and leave to chill
in the refrigerator for about
1 hour. Remove and discard the
cinnamon stick.

3 Just before serving, make the
sauce. Place the raspberries
and fruit cordial in a small
saucepan, bring to the boil and
simmer for 2–3 minutes until the
fruit is just beginning to soften.
Stir the marshmallows into the
raspberry mixture and heat
through, stirring, until the
marshmallows begin to melt.

4 Transfer the fruit salad to
serving bowls. Spoon over the
raspberry and marshmallow sauce
and serve.

VARIATION

*This sauce is delicious poured over
low-fat ice cream. For an extra-
colourful sauce, replace the
raspberries with an assortment of
summer berries.*

Brown Bread Ice Cream

*Although it sounds unusual, this yogurt-based recipe is delicious.
It contains no cream and is ideal for a low-fat diet.*

Serves 4

CALORIES PER SERVING: 265 • FAT CONTENT PER SERVING: 6 G

INGREDIENTS

175 g/6 oz fresh wholemeal
  breadcrumbs
25 g/1 oz finely chopped walnuts
60 g/2 oz caster (superfine) sugar
1/2 tsp ground nutmeg

1 tsp finely grated orange rind
450 ml/16 fl oz/2 cups low-fat
  natural (unsweetened) yogurt
2 large egg whites

TO DECORATE:
walnut halves
orange slices
fresh mint

1 Preheat the grill (broiler) to medium. Mix the breadcrumbs, walnuts and sugar together and spread over a sheet of foil in the grill (broiler) pan. Grill (broil), stirring frequently, for 5 minutes until crisp and evenly browned. (Take care that the sugar does not burn.) Remove from the heat and allow to cool.

2 When cool, transfer to a mixing bowl and mix in the nutmeg, orange rind and yogurt. In another bowl, whisk the egg whites until stiff. Gently fold into the breadcrumb mixture using a metal spoon.

3 Spoon the mixture into 4 mini-basins, smooth over the tops and freeze for 1½–2 hours until firm.

4 To serve, hold the bases of the moulds in hot water for a few seconds, then turn on to serving plates. Serve immediately, decorated with a walnut half, orange rind and fresh mint.

COOK'S TIP

If you don't have mini-basins, use ramekins or teacups or, if you prefer, use one large bowl. Alternatively, spoon the mixture into a large, freezing container to freeze and serve the ice cream in scoops.

Chocolate Cheese Pots

These super-light desserts are just the thing if you have a craving for chocolate.
They're delicious served on their own or with a selection of fruits.

Serves 4

CALORIES PER SERVING: 170 • FAT CONTENT PER SERVING: 3 G

INGREDIENTS

300 ml/¹/₂ pint/1¹/₄ cups low-fat
  natural fromage frais
  (unsweetened yogurt)
150 ml/5 fl oz/²/₃ cup low-fat
  natural (unsweetened) yogurt
25 g/1 oz icing (confectioner's) sugar

4 tsp low-fat drinking
  chocolate powder
4 tsp cocoa powder
1 tsp vanilla essence (extract)
2 tbsp dark rum (optional)
2 medium egg whites

4 chocolate cake decorations

TO SERVE:
pieces of kiwi fruit, orange and
  banana
strawberries and raspberries

1 Combine the fromage frais (unsweetened yogurt) and low-fat yogurt in a mixing bowl. Sift in the sugar, drinking chocolate and cocoa powder and mix well. Add the vanilla essence (extract) and rum, if using.

2 In another bowl, whisk the egg whites until stiff. Using a metal spoon, fold the egg whites into the fromage frais (unsweetened yogurt) and chocolate mixture.

3 Spoon the fromage frais (unsweetened yogurt) and chocolate mixture into 4 small china dessert pots and leave to chill in the refrigerator for about 30 minutes. Decorate each chocolate cheese pot with a chocolate cake decoration.

4 Serve each chocolate cheese pot with an assortment of fresh fruit, such as pieces of kiwi fruit, orange and banana, and a few whole strawberries and raspberries.

VARIATION

This chocolate mixture would make an excellent filling for a cheesecake. Make the base out of crushed Amaretti di Saronno biscuits and egg white, and set the filling with 2 tsp powdered gelatine dissolved in 2 tbsp boiling water. Make sure you use biscuits made from apricot kernels, which are virtually fat free.

Citrus Meringue Crush

This is an excellent way to use up left-over meringue shells. It is very simple to prepare, yet tastes very luxurious. Serve with a spoonful of tangy fruit sauce.

Serves 4

CALORIES PER SERVING: 195 • FAT CONTENT PER SERVING: 0.6 G

INGREDIENTS

8 ready-made meringue nests
300 ml/¹/₂ pint/1¹/₄ cups low-fat
  natural (unsweetened) yogurt
¹/₂ tsp finely grated orange rind
¹/₂ tsp finely grated lemon rind
¹/₂ tsp finely grated lime rind
2 tbsp orange liqueur or
  unsweetened orange juice

TO DECORATE:
sliced kumquat
lime rind, grated

SAUCE:
60 g/2 oz kumquats
8 tbsp unsweetened orange juice
2 tbsp lemon juice

2 tbsp lime juice
2 tbsp water
2–3 tsp caster (superfine) sugar
1 tsp cornflour (cornstarch) mixed
  with 1 tbsp water

1 Place the meringues in a clean plastic bag, seal the bag and using a rolling pin, crush the meringues into small pieces. Transfer the crushed meringues to a mixing bowl.

2 Stir the yogurt, grated citrus rinds and the liqueur or juice into the crushed meringue. Spoon the mixture into 4 mini-basins, smooth over the tops and freeze for 1½–2 hours until firm.

3 Meanwhile, make the sauce. Thinly slice the kumquats and place them in a small saucepan with the fruit juices and water. Bring gently to the boil and then simmer over a low heat for 3–4 minutes until the kumquats have just softened.

4 Sweeten with sugar to taste, stir in the cornflour (cornstarch) mixture and cook, stirring, until thickened. Pour into a small bowl, cover the surface with a layer of cling film (plastic wrap) and allow to cool – the film will help prevent a skin forming. Leave to chill until required.

5 To serve, dip the meringue basins in hot water for 5 seconds or until they loosen, and turn on to serving plates. Spoon over a little sauce, decorate with slices of kumquat and lime rind and serve immediately.

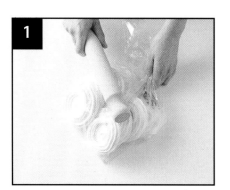

Tropical Fruit Fool

Fruit fools are always popular, and this lightly tangy version will be no exception. Use your favourite fruits in this recipe if you prefer.

Serves 4

CALORIES PER SERVING: 170 • FAT CONTENT PER SERVING: 0.6 G

INGREDIENTS

1 medium ripe mango
2 kiwi fruit
1 medium banana
2 tbsp lime juice

1/2 tsp finely grated lime rind, plus
   extra to decorate
2 medium egg whites
425 g/15 oz can low-fat custard

1/2 tsp vanilla essence (extract)
2 passion fruit

1 To peel the mango, slice either side of the smooth, flat central stone. Roughly chop the flesh and blend the fruit in a food processor or blender until smooth. Alternatively, mash with a fork.

2 Peel the kiwi fruit, chop the flesh into small pieces and place in a bowl. Peel and chop the banana and add to the bowl. Toss all of the fruit in the lime juice and rind and mix well.

3 In a grease-free bowl, whisk the egg whites until stiff and then gently fold in the custard and vanilla essence (extract) until thoroughly mixed.

4 In 4 tall glasses, alternately layer the chopped fruit, mango purée and custard mixture, finishing with the custard on top. Leave to chill in the refrigerator for 20 minutes.

5 Halve the passion fruits, scoop out the seeds and spoon the passion fruit over the fruit fools. Decorate each serving with the extra lime rind and serve.

VARIATION

Other tropical fruits to try include papaya purée, with chopped pineapple and dates, and tamarillo or pomegranate seeds to decorate. Or make a summer fruit fool by using strawberry purée, topped with raspberries and blackberries, with cherries to finish.

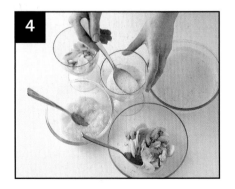

Brown Sugar Pavlovas

This simple combination of fudgey meringue topped with fromage frais (yogurt) and raspberries is the perfect finale to any meal.

Serves 4

CALORIES PER SERVING: 170 • FAT CONTENT PER SERVING: 0.2 G

INGREDIENTS

2 large egg whites
1 tsp cornflour (cornstarch)
1 tsp raspberry vinegar
100 g/3¹/₂ oz light muscovado sugar,
   crushed free of lumps

150 ml/5 fl oz/³/₄ cup low-fat
   natural fromage frais
   (unsweetened yogurt)
175 g/6 oz raspberries, thawed
   if frozen

2 tbsp redcurrant jelly
2 tbsp unsweetened orange juice
rose-scented geranium leaves,
   to decorate

1 Preheat the oven to 150°C/ 300°F/Gas Mark 2. Line a large baking sheet with baking parchment. In a large, grease-free bowl, whisk the egg whites until very stiff and dry. Fold in the cornflour (cornstarch) and vinegar.

2 Gradually whisk in the sugar, a spoonful at a time, until the mixture is thick and glossy.

3 Divide the mixture into 4 and spoon on to the baking sheet, spaced well apart. Smooth each into a round, about 10 cm/4 inch across, and bake in the oven for 40–45 minutes until lightly browned and crisp. Leave to cool on the baking tray.

4 Place the redcurrant jelly and orange juice in a small pan and heat, stirring, until melted. Leave to cool for 10 minutes.

5 Meanwhile, using a palette knife, carefully remove each pavlova from the baking parchment and transfer to a serving plate. Top with fromage frais (unsweetened yogurt) and raspberries.

6 Spoon over the redcurrant jelly mixture to glaze. Decorate and serve.

VARIATION

Make a large pavlova by forming the meringue into a round, measuring 18 cm/7 inches across, on a lined baking sheet and bake for 1 hour.

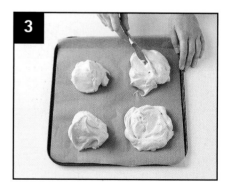

Apricot & Orange Jellies

These bright fruity little desserts are easy to make and taste so much better than shop-bought jellies. Serve them with low-fat ice cream or a home-made whip.

Serves 4

CALORIES PER SERVING: 220 • FAT CONTENT PER SERVING: 4.5 G

INGREDIENTS

225 g/8 oz no-need-to-soak
  dried apricots
300 ml/$\frac{1}{2}$ pint/$1\frac{1}{4}$ cups
  unsweetened orange juice
2 tbsp lemon juice
2–3 tsp clear honey

1 tbsp powdered gelatine
4 tbsp boiling water

TO DECORATE:
orange segments
sprigs of mint

CINNAMON 'CREAM':
115 g/4 oz medium fat ricotta cheese
115 g/4 oz low-fat natural fromage
  frais (unsweetened yogurt)
1 tsp ground cinnamon
1 tbsp clear honey

1 Place the apricots in a saucepan and pour in the orange juice. Bring to the boil, cover and simmer for 15–20 minutes until plump and soft. Leave to cool for 10 minutes.

2 Transfer the mixture to a blender or food processor and blend until smooth. Stir in the lemon juice and add the honey. Pour the mixture into a measuring jug and make up to 600 ml/1 pint /2½ cups with cold water.

3 Dissolve the gelatine in the boiling water and stir into the apricot mixture.

4 Pour the mixture into 4 individual moulds, each 150 ml/5 fl oz/⅔ cup, or 1 large mould, 600 ml/1 pint/2½ cups. Leave to chill until set.

5 Meanwhile, make the cinnamon 'cream'. Mix all the ingredients together and place in a small bowl. Cover and leave to chill.

6 To turn out the jellies, dip the moulds in hot water for a few seconds to loosen and invert on to serving plates. Decorate and serve with the cinnamon 'cream' dusted with extra cinnamon.

VARIATION

Other fruits that would work well in this recipe instead of the apricots are dried peaches, mangoes and pears.

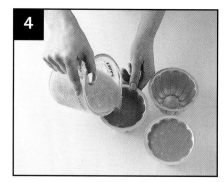

Sticky Sesame Bananas

*These tasty morsels are a real treat. Pieces of banana are dipped
in caramel and then sprinkled with a few sesame seeds.*

Serves 4

CALORIES PER SERVING: 300 • FAT CONTENT PER SERVING: 4.5 G

INGREDIENTS

4 ripe medium bananas
3 tbsp lemon juice
115 g/4 oz caster (superfine) sugar
4 tbsp cold water

2 tbsp sesame seeds
150 ml/5 fl oz/²/3 cup low-fat
  natural fromage frais
  (unsweetened yogurt)

1 tbsp icing (confectioner's) sugar
1 tsp vanilla essence (extract)
lemon and lime rind, shredded,
  to decorate

1 Peel the bananas and cut into 5 cm/2 inch pieces. Place the banana pieces in a bowl, spoon over the lemon juice and stir well to coat – this will help prevent the bananas from discolouring.

2 Place the sugar and water in a small saucepan and heat gently, stirring, until the sugar dissolves. Bring to the boil and cook for 5–6 minutes until the mixture turns golden-brown.

3 Meanwhile, drain the bananas and blot with absorbent kitchen paper to dry. Line a baking sheet or board with baking parchment and arrange the bananas, well spaced out, on top.

4 When the caramel is ready, drizzle it over the bananas, working quickly because the caramel sets almost instantly. Sprinkle over the sesame seeds and leave to cool for 10 minutes.

5 Meanwhile, mix the fromage frais (unsweetened yogurt) with the icing (confectioner's) sugar and vanilla essence (extract).

6 Peel the bananas away from the paper and arrange on serving plates. Serve the fromage frais (unsweetened yogurt) as a dip, decorated with the shredded lemon and lime rind.

COOK'S TIP

For best results, use a cannelle knife or a potato peeler to peel away thin strips of rind from the fruit, taking care not to include any bitter pith. Blanch the shreds in boiling water for 1 minute, then refresh in cold water.

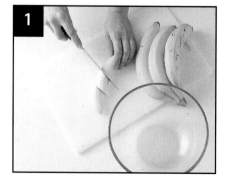

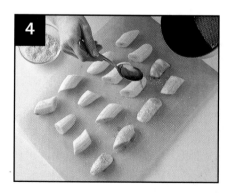

Mocha Swirl Mousse

A combination of feather-light yet rich chocolate and coffee mousses, whipped and set in serving glasses. These are definitely for a special occasion.

Serves 4

CALORIES PER SERVING: 130 • FAT CONTENT PER SERVING: 6.5 G

INGREDIENTS

1 tbsp coffee and chicory essence

2 tsp cocoa powder, plus extra for dusting

1 tsp low-fat drinking chocolate powder

150 ml/5 fl oz/²/₃ cup half-fat crème fraîche, plus 4 tsp to serve (see Cook's Tip, below)

2 tsp powdered gelatine

2 tbsp boiling water

2 large egg whites

2 tbsp caster (superfine) sugar

4 chocolate coffee beans, to serve

1 Place the coffee and chicory essence in one bowl, and 2 tsp cocoa powder and the drinking chocolate in another bowl. Divide the crème fraîche between the 2 bowls and mix both until well combined.

2 Dissolve the gelatine in the boiling water and set aside. In a grease-free bowl, whisk the egg whites and sugar until stiff and divide this mixture evenly between the coffee and chocolate mixtures.

3 Divide the dissolved gelatine between the 2 mixtures and, using a large metal spoon, gently fold until well mixed.

4 Spoon small amounts of the 2 mousses alternately into 4 serving glasses and swirl together gently. Chill for 1 hour or until set.

5 To serve, top each mousse with a teaspoonful of crème fraîche, a chocolate coffee bean and a light dusting of cocoa powder. Serve immediately.

COOK'S TIP

Traditional crème fraîche is soured cream and has a fat content of around 40 per cent. It is thick and has a slightly sour and nutty flavour. Lower fat versions have a reduced fat content and are slightly looser in texture, but they should be used in a low-fat diet only occasionally. If you want to use a lower fat alternative, a reduced fat, unsweetened yogurt or fromage frais would be more suitable.

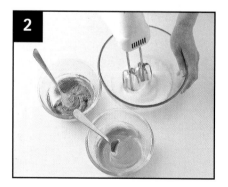

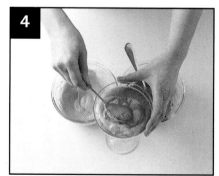

Fruit & Fibre Layers

A good, hearty dessert, guaranteed to fill you up.
Use your own favourite dried fruits in the compote.

Serves 4

CALORIES PER SERVING: 340 • FAT CONTENT PER SERVING: 6 G

INGREDIENTS

115 g/4 oz no-need-to-soak
   dried apricots
115 g/4 oz no-need-to-soak
   dried prunes
115 g/4 oz no-need-to-soak
   dried peaches

60g /2 oz dried apple
25 g/1 oz dried cherries
450 ml/16 fl oz/2 cups unsweetened
   apple juice
6 cardamom pods
6 cloves

1 cinnamon stick, broken
300 ml/$^1/_2$ pint/1$^1/_4$ cups low-fat
   natural yogurt
115 g/4 oz crunchy oat cereal
apricot slices, to decorate

1 To make the fruit compote, place the dried apricots, prunes, peaches, apples and cherries in a saucepan and pour in the apple juice.

2 Add the cardamom pods, cloves and cinnamon stick to the pan, bring to the boil and simmer for 10–15 minutes until the fruits are plump and tender.

3 Allow the mixture to cool completely in the pan, then transfer the mixture to a bowl and leave to chill in the refrigerator for 1 hour. Remove and discard the spices from the fruits.

4 Spoon the compote into 4 dessert glasses, layering it alternately with yogurt and oat cereal, finishing with the oat cereal on top.

5 Decorate each dessert with slices of apricot and serve at once.

COOK'S TIP

There are many dried fruits available, including mangoes and pears, some of which need soaking, so read the instructions on the packet before use. Also, check the ingredients label, because several types of dried fruit have added sugar or are rolled in sugar, and this will affect the sweetness of the dish that you use them in.

Pan-cooked Apples in Red Wine

This simple combination of apples and raspberries cooked in red wine is a colourful and tempting dessert.

Serves 4

CALORIES PER SERVING: 200 • FAT CONTENT PER SERVING: 4.5 G

INGREDIENTS

4 eating (dessert) apples
2 tbsp lemon juice
40 g/1¹/₂ oz low-fat spread
60 g/2 oz light muscovado sugar

1 small orange
1 cinnamon stick, broken
150 ml/5 fl oz/²/₃ cup red wine
225 g/8 oz raspberries, hulled and
  thawed if frozen

sprigs of fresh mint, to decorate

1 Peel and core the apples, then cut them into thick wedges. Place the apples in a bowl and toss in the lemon juice to prevent the fruit from discolouring.

2 In a frying pan (skillet), gently melt the low-fat spread over a low heat, add the sugar and stir to form a paste.

3 Stir the apple wedges into the pan and cook, stirring, for 2 minutes until well coated in the sugar paste.

4 Using a vegetable peeler, pare off a few strips of orange rind. Add the orange rind to the pan along with the cinnamon pieces. Extract the juice from the orange and pour into the pan with the red wine. Bring to the boil, then simmer for 10 minutes, stirring.

5 Add the raspberries to the pan and cook for 5 minutes until the apples are tender.

6 Discard the orange rind and cinnamon pieces. Transfer the apple and raspberry mixture to a serving plate together with the wine sauce. Decorate with a sprig of fresh mint and serve hot.

VARIATION

For other fruity combinations, cook the apples with blackberries, blackcurrants or redcurrants. You may need to add more sugar if you use currants as they are not as sweet as raspberries.

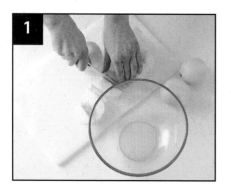

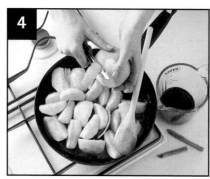

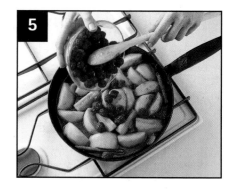

Mixed Fruit Brûlées

*Traditionally a rich mixture made with cream, this fruit-based version is
just as tempting. If you prefer, use natural (unsweetened) yogurt as a topping.*

Serves 4

CALORIES PER SERVING: 225 • FAT CONTENT PER SERVING: 11 G

INGREDIENTS

450 g/1 lb prepared, assorted
  summer fruits (such as
  strawberries, raspberries,
  blackcurrants, redcurrants and
  cherries), thawed if frozen

150 ml/5 fl oz/³/₄ cup half-fat double
  (heavy) cream alternative
150 ml/5 fl oz/³/₄ cup low-fat
  natural fromage frais
  (unsweetened yogurt)

1 tsp vanilla essence (extract)
4 tbsp demerara (brown crystal)
  sugar

1 Divide the strawberries,
raspberries, blackcurrants,
redcurrants and cherries evenly
among 4 small, heatproof
ramekin dishes.

2 Mix together the half-fat
cream alternative, fromage
frais (unsweetened yogurt) and
vanilla essence (extract).
Generously spoon the mixture
over the fruit.

3 Preheat the grill (broiler) to
hot. Top each serving with

1 tbsp demerara (brown crystal)
sugar and grill (broil) the desserts
for 2–3 minutes, until the sugar
melts and begins to caramelize.
Serve hot.

VARIATION

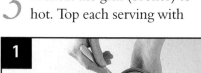

*If you are making this
dessert for a special
occasion, soak the fruits in
2–3 tbsp fruit liqueur before
topping with the cream mixture.*

COOK'S TIP

*Look out for half-fat creams, in
single and double (light and heavy)
varieties. They are good substitutes
for occasional use. Alternatively, in
this recipe, omit the cream and
double the quantity of fromage frais
(yogurt) for a lower fat version.*

Grilled Fruit Platter with Lime 'Butter'

This delicious variation of a hot fruit salad includes wedges of tropical fruits, dusted with dark brown, treacly sugar and a pinch of spice before grilling.

Serves 4

CALORIES PER SERVING: 220 • FAT CONTENT PER SERVING: 6.5 G

INGREDIENTS

1 baby pineapple
1 ripe papaya
1 ripe mango
2 kiwi fruit
4 apple (finger) bananas

4 tbsp dark rum
1 tsp ground allspice
2 tbsp lime juice
4 tbsp dark muscovado sugar

LIME 'BUTTER':
60 g/2 oz low-fat spread
$1/2$ tsp finely grated lime rind
1 tbsp icing (confectioner's) sugar

1 Quarter the pineapple, trimming away most of the leaves, and place in a shallow dish. Peel the papaya, cut it in half and scoop out the seeds. Cut the flesh into thick wedges and place in the same dish as the pineapple.

2 Peel the mango, cut either side of the smooth, central flat stone and remove the stone. Slice the flesh into thick wedges. Peel the kiwi fruit and cut in half. Peel the bananas. Add all of these fruits to the dish.

3 Sprinkle over the rum, allspice and lime juice, cover and leave at room temperature for 30 minutes, turning occasionally, to allow the flavours to develop.

4 Meanwhile, make the 'butter'. Place the low-fat spread in a small bowl and beat in the lime rind and sugar until well mixed. Leave to chill until required.

5 Preheat the grill (broiler) to hot. Drain the fruit, reserving the juices, and arrange in the grill (broiler) pan. Sprinkle with the sugar and grill (broil) for 3–4 minutes until hot, bubbling and just beginning to char.

6 Transfer the fruit to a serving plate and spoon over the juices. Serve with the lime 'butter'.

VARIATION

Serve with a light sauce of 300 ml/ $1/2$ pint/$1^1/4$ cups tropical fruit juice thickened with 2 tsp arrowroot.

Baked Pears with Cinnamon & Brown Sugar

This simple recipe is easy to prepare and cook but is deliciously warming. Serve hot with low-fat custard, or allow to cool and serve chilled with fromage frais or yogurt.

Serves 4

CALORIES PER SERVING: 160 • FAT CONTENT PER SERVING: 6 G

INGREDIENTS

4 ripe pears
2 tbsp lemon juice
4 tbsp light muscovado sugar

1 tsp ground cinnamon
60 g/2 oz low-fat spread
low-fat custard, to serve

lemon rind, finely grated, to decorate

1 Preheat the oven to 200°C/ 400°F/Gas Mark 6. Core and peel the pears, then slice them in half lengthwise and brush all over with the lemon juice to prevent the pears from discolouring. Place the pears, cored side down, in a small non-stick roasting tin (pan).

2 Place the sugar, cinnamon and low-fat spread in a small saucepan and heat gently, stirring, until the sugar has melted. Keep the heat low to stop too much water evaporating from the low-fat spread as it gets hot. Spoon the mixture over the pears.

3 Bake for 20–25 minutes or until the pears are tender and golden, occasionally spooning the sugar mixture over the fruit during the cooking time.

4 To serve, heat the custard until it is piping hot and spoon over the bases of 4 warm dessert plates. Arrange 2 pear halves on each plate. Decorate with grated lemon rind and serve.

VARIATION

This recipe also works well if you use cooking apples. For alternative flavours, replace the cinnamon with ground ginger and serve the pears sprinkled with chopped stem ginger in syrup. Alternatively, use ground allspice and spoon over some warmed dark rum to serve.

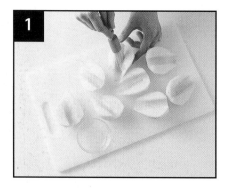

Baked Apples with Blackberries

This winter dessert is a classic dish. Large, fluffy apples are hollowed out and filled with spices, almonds and blackberries. Serve hot with low-fat custard.

Serves 4

CALORIES PER SERVING: 250 • FAT CONTENT PER SERVING: 2 G

INGREDIENTS

4 medium-sized cooking apples
1 tbsp lemon juice
100 g/3¹/₂ oz prepared blackberries,
   thawed if frozen
15 g/¹/₂ oz flaked (slivered) almonds

¹/₂ tsp ground allspice
¹/₂ tsp finely grated lemon rind
2 tbsp demerara (brown crystal)
   sugar
300 ml/¹/₂ pint/1¹/₄ cups ruby port

1 cinnamon stick, broken
2 tsp cornflour (cornstarch) blended
   with 2 tbsp cold water
low-fat custard, to serve

1 Preheat the oven to 200°C/ 400°F/Gas Mark 6. Wash and dry the apples. Using a small sharp knife, make a shallow cut through the skin around the middle of each apple – this will help the apples to cook through.

2 Core the apples, brush the centres with the lemon juice to prevent browning and stand in a shallow ovenproof dish.

3 In a bowl, mix together the blackberries, almonds, allspice, lemon rind and sugar. Using a teaspoon, spoon the mixture into the centre of each apple.

4 Pour the port into the tin, add the cinnamon stick and bake the apples in the oven for 35–40 minutes or until tender and soft. Drain the cooking juices into a pan and keep the apples warm.

5 Discard the cinnamon and add the cornflour (cornstarch) mixture to the cooking juices. Heat, stirring, until thickened.

6 Heat the custard until piping hot. Pour the sauce over the apples and serve with the custard.

VARIATION

Use raspberries instead of blackberries and, if you prefer, replace the port with unsweetened orange juice.

White Lace Crêpes with Oriental Fruits

These super-light crêpes melt in the mouth. They are filled with a gingered fruit salad of melon, grapes and lychees.

Serves 4

CALORIES PER SERVING: 170 • FAT CONTENT PER SERVING: 1.5 G

INGREDIENTS

3 medium egg whites
4 tbsp cornflour (cornstarch)
3 tbsp cold water
1 tsp vegetable oil

FILLING:
350 g/12 oz fresh lychees
$1/4$ Galia melon
175 g/6 oz seedless green grapes

1 cm/$1/2$ inch piece root (fresh) ginger
2 pieces stem ginger in syrup
2 tbsp ginger wine *or* dry sherry

1 To make the fruit filling, peel the lychees and remove the stones. Place the lychees in a bowl. Scoop out the seeds from the melon and remove the skin. Cut the melon flesh into small pieces and place in the bowl.

2 Wash and dry the grapes, remove the stalks and add to the bowl. Peel the ginger and cut into thin shreds or grate finely. Drain the stem ginger pieces, reserving the syrup, and chop the ginger pieces finely.

3 Mix the gingers into the bowl along with the ginger wine or sherry and the reserved stem ginger syrup. Cover and set aside.

4 Meanwhile, prepare the crêpes. In a small jug, mix together the egg whites, cornflour (cornstarch) and cold water until very smooth.

5 Brush a small non-stick crêpe pan with oil and heat until hot. Drizzle the surface of the pan with a quarter of the cornflour (cornstarch) mixture to give a lacy effect. Cook for a few seconds until set, then carefully lift out and transfer to absorbent kitchen paper to drain. Set aside and keep warm. Repeat with the remaining mixture to make 4 crêpes in total.

6 To serve, place a crêpe on each serving plate and top with the fruit filling. Fold over the pancake and serve hot.

Fruit Loaf with Strawberry & Apple Spread

This sweet, fruity loaf is ideal served for tea or as a healthy snack.

Serves 8

CALORIES PER SERVING: 360 • FAT CONTENT PER SERVING: 2.8 G

INGREDIENTS

175 g/6 oz porridge oats (oatmeal)
100 g/3¹/₂ oz light muscovado sugar
1 tsp ground cinnamon
125 g/4¹/₂ oz golden sultanas
175 g/6 oz seedless raisins
2 tbsp malt extract
300 ml/¹/₂ pint/1¹/₄ cups
   unsweetened apple juice

175 g/6 oz self-raising wholemeal
   (whole wheat) flour
1¹/₂ tsp baking powder
strawberries and apple wedges,
   to serve

FRUIT SPREAD:
225 g/8 oz strawberries, washed
   and hulled
2 eating (dessert) apples, cored,
   chopped and mixed with 1 tbsp
   lemon juice to prevent browning
300 ml/¹/₂ pint/1¹/₄ cups
   unsweetened apple juice

1 Preheat the oven to 180°C/ 350°F/Gas Mark 4. Grease and line a 900 g/2 lb loaf tin. Place the porridge oats (oatmeal), sugar, cinnamon, sultanas, raisins and malt extract in a mixing bowl. Pour in the apple juice, stir well and leave to soak for 30 minutes.

2 Sift in the flour and baking powder, adding any husks that remain in the sieve, and fold in using a metal spoon. Spoon the mixture into the prepared tin and bake for 1½ hours until firm or until a skewer inserted into the centre comes out clean. Leave to cool for 10 minutes, then turn on to a rack and leave to cool completely.

3 Meanwhile, make the fruit spread. Place the strawberries and apples in a saucepan and pour in the apple juice. Bring to the boil, cover and simmer for 30 minutes. Beat the sauce well and spoon into a clean, warmed jar. Leave to cool, then seal and label.

4 Serve the loaf with 1–2 tablespoons of the fruit spread and an assortment of strawberries and apple wedges.

Banana & Lime Cake

A substantial loaf-type cake that is ideal served for tea. The mashed bananas help to keep the cake moist, and it is drizzled with a lime icing for extra zing and zest.

Serves 10

CALORIES PER SERVING: 360 • FAT CONTENT PER SERVING: 2.8 G

INGREDIENTS

300 g/10^1/$_2$ oz plain (all-purpose) flour
1 tsp salt
1^1/$_2$ tsp baking powder
175 g/6 oz light muscovado sugar
1 tsp lime rind, grated
1 medium egg, beaten

1 medium banana, mashed with 1 tbsp lime juice
150 ml/5 fl oz/^{2}/$_3$ cup low-fat natural fromage frais (unsweetened yogurt)
115 g/4 oz sultanas
banana chips, to decorate
lime rind, finely grated, to decorate

TOPPING:
115 g/4 oz icing (confectioner's) sugar
1–2 tsp lime juice
^{1}/$_2$ tsp lime rind, finely grated

1 Preheat the oven to 180°C/350°F/Gas Mark 4. Grease and line a deep 18 cm/7 inch round cake tin with baking parchment. Sift the flour, salt and baking powder into a mixing bowl and stir in the sugar and lime rind.

2 Make a well in the centre of the dry ingredients and add the egg, banana, fromage frais (yogurt) and sultanas. Mix well until thoroughly incorporated.

3 Spoon the mixture into the tin and smooth the surface. Bake for 40–45 minutes until firm to the touch or until a skewer inserted in the centre comes out clean. Leave to cool for 10 minutes, then turn out on to a wire rack.

4 To make the topping, sift the icing (confectioner's) sugar into a small bowl and mix with the lime juice to form a soft, but not too runny, icing. Stir in the lime rind. Drizzle the icing over the cake, letting it run down the sides.

5 Decorate with banana chips and lime rind. Let stand for 15 minutes so that the icing sets.

VARIATION

Replace the lime rind and juice with orange and the sultanas with chopped apricots.

Crispy Sugar-topped Blackberry & Apple Cake

The sugar cubes give a lovely crunchy top to this moist bake.

Serves 10

CALORIES PER SERVING: 230 • FAT CONTENT PER SERVING: 1.5 G

INGREDIENTS

350 g/12 oz cooking apples
3 tbsp lemon juice
300 g/10 1/2 oz self-raising
   wholemeal (whole wheat) flour
1/2 tsp baking powder
1 tsp ground cinnamon, plus extra
   for dusting

175 g/6 oz prepared blackberries,
   thawed if frozen, plus extra to
   decorate
175 g/6 oz light muscovado sugar
1 medium egg, beaten

200 ml/7 fl oz/3/4 cup low-fat
   natural fromage frais
   (unsweetened yogurt)
60 g/2 oz white or brown sugar
   cubes, lightly crushed
sliced eating (dessert) apple,
   to decorate

1 Preheat the oven to 190°C/
375°F/Gas Mark 5. Grease
and line a 900 g/2 lb loaf tin. Core,
peel and finely dice the apples.
Place them in a saucepan with the
lemon juice, bring to the boil,
cover and simmer for 10 minutes
until soft and pulpy. Beat well and
set aside to cool.

2 Sift the flour, baking powder
and 1 tsp cinnamon into a
bowl, adding any husks that
remain in the sieve. Stir in 115 g/
4 oz blackberries and the sugar.

3 Make a well in the centre of
the ingredients and add the
egg, fromage frais (unsweetened
yogurt) and cooled apple purée.
Mix well to incorporate
thoroughly. Spoon the mixture
into the prepared loaf tin and
smooth over the top.

4 Sprinkle with the remaining
blackberries, pressing them
down into the cake mixture, and
top with the crushed sugar lumps.
Bake for 40–45 minutes. Leave to
cool in the tin.

5 Remove the cake from the tin
and peel away the lining
paper. Serve dusted with
cinnamon and decorated with
extra blackberries and apple slices.

Rich Fruit Cake

This moist cake would also make an excellent Christmas cake.

Serves 12

CALORIES PER SERVING: 315 • FAT CONTENT PER SERVING: 3 G

INGREDIENTS

175 g/6 oz unsweetened pitted dates
115 g/4 oz no-need-to-soak
  dried prunes
200 ml/7 fl oz/³/₄ cup unsweetened
  orange juice
2 tbsp treacle (molasses)
1 tsp finely grated lemon rind
1 tsp finely grated orange rind

225 g/8 oz self-raising wholemeal
  (whole wheat) flour
1 tsp mixed spice
115 g/4 oz seedless raisins
115 g/4 oz golden sultanas
115 g/4 oz currants
115 g/4 oz dried cranberries
3 large eggs, separated

icing (confectioner's) sugar

TO DECORATE:
1 tbsp apricot jam, softened
175 g/6 oz sugarpaste
strips of orange rind
strips of lemon rind

1 Preheat the oven to 170°C/ 325°F/Gas Mark 3. Grease and line a deep 20.5 cm/8 inch round cake tin. Chop the dates and prunes and place in a pan. Pour over the orange juice and bring to the boil. Simmer for 10 minutes until very soft.

2 Remove the pan from the heat and beat the fruit mixture until puréed. Stir in the treacle (molasses) and citrus rinds. Leave to cool.

3 Meanwhile, sift the flour and mixed spice into a bowl, adding any husks that remain in the sieve. Mix in the dried fruits and make a well in the centre.

4 When the date and prune mixture is cool, whisk in the egg yolks. In a separate bowl, whisk the egg whites until stiff. Spoon the fruit and egg yolk mixture into the dry ingredients and gradually work together using a wooden spoon.

5 Gently fold in the egg whites using a metal spoon. Transfer to the prepared tin and bake for 1½ hours. Leave to cool in the tin.

6 Remove the cake from the tin and brush the top with jam. Dust the work surface (counter) with icing (confectioner's) sugar and roll out the sugarpaste thinly. Lay the sugarpaste over the top of the cake and trim the edges. Decorate the cake with orange and lemon rind.

Carrot & Ginger Cake

This melt-in-the-mouth version has a fraction of the fat of the traditional cake.

Serves 10

CALORIES PER SERVING: 300 • FAT CONTENT PER SERVING: 10 G

INGREDIENTS

225 g/8 oz plain (all-purpose) flour
1 tsp baking powder
1 tsp bicarbonate of soda
2 tsp ground ginger
1/2 tsp salt
175 g/6 oz light muscovado sugar
225 g/8 oz carrots, grated
2 pieces stem ginger in syrup,
   drained and chopped
25 g/1 oz root (fresh) ginger, grated

60 g/2 oz seedless raisins
2 medium eggs, beaten
3 tbsp corn oil
juice of 1 medium orange

TO DECORATE:
grated carrot
stem (fresh) ginger
ground ginger

FROSTING:
225 g/8 oz low-fat soft cheese
4 tbsp icing (confectioner's) sugar
1 tsp vanilla essence (extract)

1 Preheat the oven to 180°C/
350°F/Gas Mark 4. Grease
and line a 20.5 cm/8 inch round
cake tin with baking parchment.

2 Sift the flour, baking powder,
bicarbonate of soda, ground
ginger and salt into a mixing bowl.
Stir in the sugar, carrot, stem
ginger, root (fresh) ginger and
raisins. Make a well in the centre
of the dry ingredients.

3 Beat together the eggs, oil and
orange juice, then pour into
the centre of the well. Combine
the ingredients together until
well mixed.

4 Spoon the mixture into the
tin and smooth the surface.
Bake in the oven for 1–1 1/4 hours
until firm to the touch, or until a
skewer inserted into the centre
comes out clean. Cool in the tin.

5 To make the frosting, place
the soft cheese in a bowl and
beat to soften. Sift in the icing
(confectioner's) sugar and add the
vanilla essence (extract). Stir well
to mix.

6 Remove the cake from the tin
and smooth the frosting over
the top. Serve decorated with
grated carrot, stem ginger and a
dusting of ground ginger.

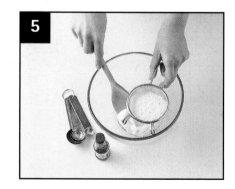

Strawberry Roulade

The light, moist sponge rolled up with an almond and strawberry fromage frais (yogurt) filling is not strictly a roulade – it contains flour – but the result is similar.

Serves 8

CALORIES PER SERVING: 185 • FAT CONTENT PER SERVING: 4 G

INGREDIENTS

3 large eggs
115 g/4 oz caster (superfine) sugar
115 g/4 oz plain (all-purpose) flour
1 tbsp hot water

FILLING:
200 ml/7 fl oz/^{3}/$_4$ cup low-fat natural
  fromage frais (unsweetened
  yogurt)
1 tsp almond essence (extract)

225 g/8 oz small strawberries
15 g/^{1}/$_2$ oz toasted almonds,
  flaked (slivered)
1 tsp icing (confectioner's) sugar

1 Preheat the oven to 220°C/ 425°F/Gas Mark 7. Line a 35 x 25 cm/14 x 10 inch Swiss roll tin with baking parchment. Place the eggs in a mixing bowl with the caster (superfine) sugar. Place the bowl over a pan of hot water and whisk until pale and thick.

2 Remove the bowl from the pan. Sift in the flour and fold into the eggs with the hot water. Pour the mixture into the tin and bake for 8–10 minutes, until golden and set.

3 Transfer the mixture to a sheet of baking parchment. Peel off the lining paper and roll up the sponge tightly along with the baking parchment. Wrap in a tea towel (dish towel) and let cool.

4 To make the filling, mix together the fromage frais (yogurt) and almond essence (extract). Reserving a few strawberries for decoration, wash, hull and slice the rest. Leave the filling mixture to chill until ready to assemble.

5 Unroll the sponge, spread the fromage frais (yogurt) mixture over the sponge and sprinkle with strawberries. Roll the sponge up again and transfer to a serving plate. Sprinkle with the almonds and lightly dust with icing (confectioner's) sugar. Decorate with the reserved strawberries.

VARIATION

Serve the roulade with a fruit purée, sweetened with a little sugar.

Fruity Muffins

Another American favourite, these little cakes contain no butter, just a little corn oil.

Makes 10

CALORIES PER SERVING: 180 • FAT CONTENT PER SERVING: 1.5 G

INGREDIENTS

225 g/8 oz self-raising wholemeal
   (whole wheat) flour
2 tsp baking powder
25 g/1 oz light muscovado sugar
100 g/3^1/$_2$ oz no-need-to-soak dried
   apricots, chopped finely

1 medium banana, mashed with
   1 tbsp orange juice
1 tsp orange rind, grated finely
300 ml/^{1}/$_2$ pint/1^1/$_4$ cups
   skimmed milk
1 medium egg, beaten

3 tbsp corn oil
2 tbsp porridge oats (oatmeal)
fruit spread, honey or maple syrup,
   to serve

1 Preheat the oven to 200°C/ 400°F/Gas Mark 6. Place 10 paper muffin cases in a deep patty tin (pan).

2 Sift the flour and baking powder into a mixing bowl, adding any husks that remain in the sieve. Stir in the sugar and chopped apricots.

3 Make a well in the centre of the dry ingredients and add the banana, orange rind, milk, beaten egg and oil. Mix together well to form a thick batter. Divide the batter evenly among the 10 paper cases.

4 Sprinkle with a few porridge oats (oatmeal) and bake for 25–30 minutes until well risen and firm to the touch, or until a skewer inserted into the centre comes out clean. Transfer the muffins to a wire rack to cool slightly.

5 Serve the muffins warm with a little fruit spread, honey or maple syrup.

VARIATION

If you like dried figs, they make a deliciously crunchy alternative to the apricots; they also go very well with the flavour of orange. Other no-need-to-soak dried fruits, chopped up finely, can be used as well. Store these muffins in an airtight container for 3-4 days. They also freeze well in sealed bags or in freezer containers for up to 3 months.

Chocolate Brownies

Yes, you really can have a low-fat chocolate treat. These moist bars incorporate a dried fruit purée, which enables you to bake without adding any fat.

Makes 12

CALORIES PER SERVING: 300 • FAT CONTENT PER SERVING: 4.5 G

INGREDIENTS

60 g/2 oz unsweetened pitted
 dates, chopped
60 g/2 oz no-need-to-soak dried
 prunes, chopped
6 tbsp unsweetened apple juice
4 medium eggs, beaten
300 g/10½ oz dark muscovado sugar

1 tsp vanilla essence (extract)
4 tbsp low-fat drinking chocolate
 powder, plus extra for dusting
2 tbsp cocoa powder
175 g/6 oz plain (all-purpose) flour
60 g/2 oz plain chocolate chips

ICING:
115 g/4 oz icing (confectioner's)
 sugar
1–2 tsp water
1 tsp vanilla essence (extract)

1 Preheat the oven to 180°C/350°F/Gas Mark 4. Grease and line a 18 x 28 cm/7 x 11 inch cake tin with baking parchment. Place the dates and prunes in a small saucepan and add the apple juice. Bring to the boil, cover and simmer for 10 minutes until soft. Beat to form a smooth paste, then set aside to cool.

2 Place the cooled fruit in a mixing bowl and stir in the eggs, sugar and vanilla essence. Sift in 4 tbsp drinking chocolate, the cocoa and the flour, and fold in along with the chocolate chips until well incorporated.

3 Spoon the mixture into the prepared tin and smooth over the top. Bake for 25–30 minutes until firm to the touch or until a skewer inserted into the centre comes out clean. Cut into 12 bars and leave to cool in the tin for 10 minutes. Transfer to a wire rack to cool completely.

4 To make the icing, sift the sugar into a bowl and mix with sufficient water and the vanilla essence (extract) to form a soft, but not too runny, icing.

5 Drizzle the icing over the chocolate brownies and allow to set. Dust with the extra chocolate powder before serving.

Cheese & Chive Scones

These tea-time classics have been given a healthy twist by the use of low-fat soft cheese and reduced-fat Cheddar cheese. They're just as delicious, however. Serve warm for the best flavour.

Makes 10

CALORIES PER SERVING: 120 • FAT CONTENT PER SERVING: 2.8 G

INGREDIENTS

250 g/9 oz self-raising flour
1 tsp powdered mustard
1/2 tsp cayenne pepper
1/2 tsp salt

100 g/3 1/2 oz low-fat soft cheese
  with added herbs
2 tbsp fresh snipped chives, plus
  extra to garnish

100 ml/3 1/2 fl oz and 2 tbsp skimmed
  milk
60 g/2 oz reduced-fat Cheddar
  cheese, grated
low-fat soft cheese, to serve

1 Preheat the oven to 200°C/ 400°F/Gas Mark 6. Sift the flour, mustard, cayenne and salt into a mixing bowl.

2 Add the soft cheese to the mixture and mix together until well incorporated. Stir in the snipped chives.

3 Make a well in the centre of the ingredients and gradually pour in 100 ml/3½ fl oz milk, stirring as you pour, until the mixture forms a soft dough.

4 Turn the dough on to a floured surface and knead lightly. Roll out until 2 cm/¾ inch thick and use a 5 cm/2 inch plain pastry cutter to stamp out as many rounds as you can. Transfer the rounds to a baking sheet.

5 Re-knead the dough trimmings together and roll out again. Stamp out more rounds – you should be able to make 10 scones in total.

6 Brush the scones with the remaining milk and sprinkle

with the grated cheese. Bake in the oven for 15–20 minutes until risen and golden. Transfer to a wire rack to cool. Serve warm with low-fat soft cheese, garnished with chives.

VARIATION

For sweet scones, omit the mustard, cayenne pepper, chives and grated cheese and add 75g/3oz currants or sultanas and 25 g/1 oz sugar, and use plain low-fat soft cheese.

Savoury Tomato & (Bell) Pepper Bread

This flavoursome bread contains only the minimum amount of fat.

Serves 8

CALORIES PER SERVING: 250 • FAT CONTENT PER SERVING: 3 G

INGREDIENTS

1 small red (bell) pepper
1 small green (bell) pepper
1 small yellow (bell) pepper
60 g/2 oz dry-pack sun-dried
   tomatoes
50 ml/2 fl oz boiling water

2 tsp dried yeast
1 tsp caster (superfine) sugar
150 ml/5 fl oz/^{2}/$_3$ cup tepid water
450 g/1 lb strong white bread flour
2 tsp dried rosemary
2 tbsp tomato purée (paste)

150 ml/5 fl oz/^{2}/$_3$ cup low-fat
   natural fromage frais
   (unsweetened yogurt)
1 tbsp coarse salt
1 tbsp olive oil

1 Preheat the oven to 220°C/ 425°F/Gas Mark 7 and the grill (broiler) to hot. Halve and deseed the (bell) peppers, arrange on the grill (broiler) rack and cook until the skin is charred. Leave to cool for 10 minutes, peel off the skin and chop the flesh.

2 Slice the tomatoes into strips, place in a heatproof bowl and pour over the boiling water. Set aside to soak.

3 Place the yeast and sugar in a small jug, pour over the water

and leave for 10–15 minutes until frothy. Sift the flour into a bowl and add 1 tsp dried rosemary. Make a well in the centre and pour in the yeast mixture.

4 Add the tomato purée (paste), the tomatoes and soaking liquid, the (bell) peppers, fromage frais (yogurt) and half the salt. Mix together to form a soft dough.

5 Turn the dough out on to a lightly floured surface and knead for 3–4 minutes until smooth and elastic. Place in a

lightly floured bowl, cover and leave in a warm room for about 40 minutes until doubled in size.

6 Knead the dough again and place in a lightly greased 23 cm/9 inch round spring-clip cake tin. Using a wooden spoon, form 'dimples' in the surface. Cover and leave for 30 minutes.

7 Brush with oil and sprinkle with rosemary and salt. Bake for 35–40 minutes, cool for 10 minutes and release from the tin. Leave to cool on a rack and serve.

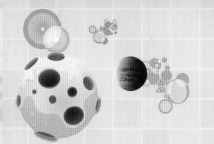
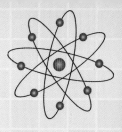

Contents

Introduction

How many different building blocks does it take to make a cell? Or a stone? Or a star? You might think it would be hundreds or even thousands, but actually it's far fewer.

But maybe that's not really such a surprise. After all, think how many different creations you can make from only a few building bricks. The 'building bricks' of the universe are called elements. There are only 92 of them, but there are millions of possible compounds you can make from them.

Have you ever wanted to know which metal screams when you bend it? Or which one is so reactive it can make glass burst into flames? Do you want to discover which are the most poisonous and which are the most radioactive elements?

Then read on...

What are the Elements?

An element is a substance that can't be broken down into a simpler substance by any sort of chemical reaction. It only contains one type of atom. There are 92 different elements that occur naturally, and some more that can only be made in a laboratory. Chemists have discovered that some of these man-made elements do actually occur naturally, but only in tiny amounts. However, we're going to stick with the original 92 in this book.

Chemists started to identify elements hundreds of years ago, and by the middle of the 1800s, 57 were known. Nobody could agree on how they should be grouped together. Someone needed to take charge and sort things out…

It was a job for Professor Mendeleev.

Dmitri Mendeleev

was born in 1834 in Siberia, the youngest of 14, or possibly even 17 children (perhaps they all kept moving around when their parents tried to count them)! When Mendeleev grew up he taught Chemistry at St Petersburg University. In photos he looks like a real mad scientist — supposedly he only cut his hair and beard once a year!

Reihen	Gruppo I. R'O	Gruppo II. RO	Gruppo III. R²O³	Gruppo IV. RH⁴ RO²	Gruppo V. RH³ R²O⁵	Gruppo VI. RH² RO³	Gruppo VII. RH R²O'	Gruppo VIII. RO⁴
1	H=1							
2	Li=7	Be=9,4	B=11	C=12	N	O=16	F=19	
3	Na=23	Mg=24	Al=27,8	Si=	P=31	S=S	Cl=35,5	
4	K=39	Ca=40	—=44	Ti=48	—51	Cr=52	=55	Fe=56, Co=59, Ni=59, Cu=63.
5	(Cu=63)	Zn=65	—=68	—=72	As=75	Se=	=80	
6	Rb=85	Sr=87	?Yt=88	Zr=	=94	Mo=96	=100	Ru=104, Rh=104, Pd=106, Ag=108.
7	(Ag=108)	Cd=112	In=113				=127	
8	Cs=133	Ba=137	?Di=138	?Ce=				
9	(—)							
10	—	—	?Er=178	?La=				Os=195, Ir=197, Pt=198, Au=199.
11	(Au=199)	Hg=200	Tl=204	Pb=207			—	
12	—	—	—	Th=231			—	

Professor Mendeleev's periodic table.

Professor Mendeleev's chemistry class

Mendeleev had a brilliant idea during his career, and that was to arrange the elements based on their weights and their properties (how they behaved). He called his arrangement The Periodic Table.

Mendeleev found that when he arranged them in this way there seemed to be 'families' of elements that showed similarities, and gaps in the table where no known element fitted the pattern. Mendeleev predicted that new elements would be found to fill the gaps and suggested what weights and properties they would have.

This helped other chemists to find them, and Mendeleev's predictions were proved correct.

How the Periodic Table Works

Here is the modern periodic table. Let's take a closer look...

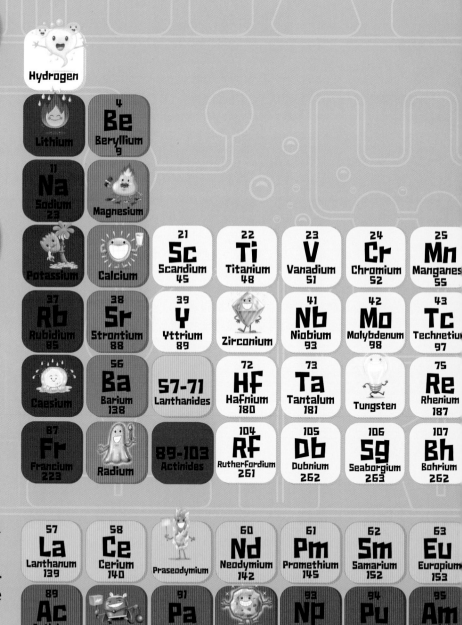

The colour of each box tells you if the element is a metal, non-metal or metalloid. The rows in the table are called periods. If you read across a period the atomic numbers of the elements increase from left to right. The columns of the table are called groups. The elements in a group have similar properties and get heavier the further down the group they are.

Hydrogen

Lithium

4
Be
Beryllium
9

11
Na
Sodium
23

Magnesium

Potassium

Calcium

21
Sc
Scandium
45

22
Ti
Titanium
48

23
V
Vanadium
51

24
Cr
Chromium
52

25
Mn
Manganese
55

37
Rb
Rubidium
85

38
Sr
Strontium
88

39
Y
Yttrium
89

Zirconium

41
Nb
Niobium
93

42
Mo
Molybdenum
98

43
Tc
Technetium
97

Caesium

56
Ba
Barium
138

57-71
Lanthanides

72
Hf
Hafnium
180

73
Ta
Tantalum
181

Tungsten

75
Re
Rhenium
187

87
Fr
Francium
223

Radium

89-103
Actinides

104
Rf
Rutherfordium
261

105
Db
Dubnium
262

106
Sg
Seaborgium
263

107
Bh
Bohrium
262

57
La
Lanthanum
139

58
Ce
Cerium
140

Praseodymium

60
Nd
Neodymium
142

61
Pm
Promethium
145

62
Sm
Samarium
152

63
Eu
Europium
153

89
Ac
Actinium
227

Thorium

91
Pa
Protactinium
231

Uranium

93
Np
Neptunium
237

94
Pu
Plutonium
244

95
Am
Americium
243

Each element has a box.
The box contains:

The atomic number
(The number of protons in an element)

The chemical symbol
(A one, two or three letter code for the element)

The name of the element

Atomic number **79**
Au
Gold

Helium

5 B Boron 11	 Carbon	 Nitrogen	Oxygen	Fluorine	10 Ne Neon 20
13 Al Aluminium 27	Silicon	15 P Phosphorus 31	Sulphur	Chlorine	Argon

Iron	Cobalt	28 Ni Nickel 58	Copper	30 Zn Zinc 64	31 Ga Gallium 69	32 Ge Germanium 74	Arsenic	Selenium	35 Br Bromine 79	36 Kr Krypton 84
44 Ru Ruthenium 102	45 Rh Rhodium 103	46 Pd Palladium 106	Silver	Cadmium	Indium	50 Sn Tin 120	Antimony	52 Te Tellurium 130	53 I Iodine 127	54 Xe Xenon 132
76 Os Osmium 192	77 Ir Iridium 193	Platinum	Gold	Mercury	81 Ti Thallium 205	Lead	Bismuth	Polonium	85 At Astatine 210	86 Rn Radon 222
108 Hs Hassium 265	109 Mt Meitnerium 266	110 Ds Darmstadtium 269	111 Rg Roentgenium 272	112 Cn Copernicium 285	113 Uut Ununtrium 286	114 Fl Flerovium 289	115 UuP Ununpentium 289	116 Lv Livermonium 293	117 Uus Ununseptium 294	118 Uno Ununoctium 294

64 Gd Gadolinium 158	65 Tb Terbium 159	66 Dy Dysprosium 164	Holmium	68 Er Erbium 168	69 Tm Thulium 169	70 Yb Ytterbium 174	71 Lu Lutetium 175	**Lanthanides**
96 Cm Curium 247	97 Bk Berkelium 247	98 Cf Californium 251	99 Es Einsteinium 254	100 Fm Fermium 257	101 Md Mandelevium 258	102 No Nobelium 255	103 Lr Lawrencium 256	**Actinides**

*There is a full periodic table on page 60 which contains all the chemical symbols.

Atoms

An atom is the smallest unit of an element and it is made up of protons, neutrons and electrons. Atoms are incredibly small – 0.000001 milimetres – and can only be seen by using a very special microscope. Their tiny size is very hard to imagine, and what makes it even harder is that most of that is empty space!

The nucleus (the centre) of an atom is made up of protons and neutrons. These make up almost all of the atom's mass. Protons have a positive charge, and the electrons whizzing round outside the nucleus have an equal negative charge. Neutrons don't have a charge.

⚛ If the whole atom was the size of a football stadium, the nucleus would be the size of a marble, and the electrons would be like tiny insects buzzing round the edge. The rest is just... nothing!

Here's how atoms are often shown:

electrons

nucleus

Let's try and understand this a different way...

Compounds and mixtures

Most substances in the world are compounds or mixtures. Compounds are made up of atoms of two or more elements joined together to form molecules. For instance, a molecule of water is an oxygen atom joined to two hydrogen atoms.

Air, on the other hand, is a mixture. It is made up of various elements like oxygen and nitrogen, together with compounds like carbon dioxide, all bobbing about together without actually being joined to each other.

Think of a mixture, like air, as a box of building bricks – they're in the box, but they're not joined together.
A compound, like water, would be building bricks joined to each other.

Solids, liquids and gases

These are what are known as the States of Matter. Chemists used to think that there were only three – solids, liquids and gases – and most things exist in one of these forms. However, there is a fourth reasonably common one called plasma (not the same as the stuff in your blood), and a whole load of what are called Exotic States of Matter that only exist in extreme laboratory conditions, or are just theoretical.

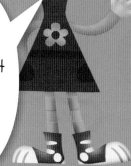

But lets get back to the basics...

Solids have a fixed shape and volume. The molecules are tightly packed meaning that they can't move around – but they do vibrate.

Liquids have a fixed volume, but take the shape of the container they are in. The molecules are tightly packed but can move a bit more than they can in a solid.

Gases have no fixed volume or shape. The molecules are not tightly packed and can move around freely.

11

Bang! Once Upon a Time...

Once upon a time, there was no universe at all, no space, no time – nothing. Then, a tiny, unbelievably hot and dense thing called a singularity appeared.

Eventually, about 13.7 billion years ago, the singularity suddenly exploded with indescribable force, and began to expand incredibly fast, in what physicists now call the Big Bang. As the singularity expanded, becoming less hot and dense, space and time came into existence and the universe was born. And it's still expanding now – galaxies are continuously moving away from each other. At that point in time, there were no elements – let alone stars or planets – just subatomic particles (loads of things that eventually form an atom). It took hundreds of thousands of years for the first atoms to form, then eventually, the first elements: hydrogen and helium – let's start with them and work our way from the lightest to the heaviest elements in the periodic table.

Atomic number 1
H
Hydrogen
Non-Metal

Hydrogen is the lightest element – its atoms each contain only one proton and one electron. It is also the most common element. At least 90% of all the atoms in the universe are hydrogen.

It was one of the first elements created by the Big Bang. Hydrogen is lighter than air, so was previously used to fill balloons and airships for air travel. Now we are beginning to use burning hydrogen as a fuel in buses, as it only produces water when it is burned, instead of the pollutants produced by burning fossil fuels.

The Hindenberg disaster

Airships filled with hydrogen were known as zeppelins. They were regularly being used to carry passengers by 1910 and were used by the German army to bomb London during World War I. Transatlantic passenger flights started in the 1920s but on May 6, 1937, disaster struck when the Hindenberg airship burned and crashed in New Jersey after flying from Frankfurt, killing 35 of the 97 people on board. It was the end of airship travel. It was assumed for a long time that the crash was caused by burning hydrogen, but now there are other theories. One of these is that flammable paint on the airship 'skin' was the first thing to catch fire, with the hydrogen burning later.

Crash of the *Hindenburg* in New Jersey, May 1937.

Burning stars

The sun is mostly made of hydrogen. Sunlight? That's the visible energy released when hydrogen is turned into helium by a process called nuclear fusion, which releases huge amounts of energy.

13

Atomic number 2

He
Helium
Non-Metal

Helium was identified in space before it was found on Earth, in 1882 by a scientist studying lava from Vesuvius. It was created in the Big Bang and is lighter than air, which is why helium party balloons float.

Although it is the second most abundant element in the universe, making up almost a quarter of its mass, it's quite rare on Earth – most of it comes from natural gas – and in fact we are running out of it! The molecules are so tiny that whenever any is released, it just floats off into space. Helium is also used in the manufacture of mobile phones and computer chips, as a super coolant in the Large Hadron Collider, and as part of the gas mixture breathed by deep-sea divers.

Breathing helium

If you have a helium party balloon ask an adult if you can try the following experiment.

🎈 Untie the balloon carefully, breathe out, then take a breath of helium from the balloon. Now try talking and you'll find your voice has gone very squeaky!

🎈 Make sure you breathe normal air for a few minutes before you try it again so you don't get dizzy.

Why does your voice change? It's because the sound waves made by your vocal cords vibrating are travelling through helium, not air, and because helium is much lighter than air, they travel faster.

The Noble Gases

Non-metals

These are the elements in the same column or group of the periodic table as **helium**.

They are		
Neon	Ne	Atomic number 10
Argon	Ar	Atomic number 18
Krypton	Kr	Atomic number 36
Xenon	Xe	Atomic number 54
Radon	Rn	Atomic number 86

10
Ne
Neon

18
Ar
Argon

Kr
Krypton

54
Xe
Xenon

86
Rn
Radon

They are called the Noble Gases, because they are so unreactive – they don't like to have anything to do with any other elements. In fact neon doesn't form any chemical compounds at all. They should really be called the Stuck Up Gases!

They are used in various sorts of lighting. Argon was used in old-fashioned light bulbs and is still used in fluorescent tubes.

The gases have medical uses too – xenon is used as an anaesthetic and radioactive radon is used as a cancer treatment.

Krypton and Kryptonite

Don't confuse krypton with Kryptonite! Kryptonite, which drains Superman of his powers, is a fictional element from Superman's home planet, Krypton. As far as we know krypton is just a gas, not a planet!

Atomic number 6

C
Carbon
Non-Metal

All life on Earth is based on chemicals that contain carbon. It can join with other elements to form millions of different compounds. Pure carbon can exist in several different forms: graphite (which is the 'lead' in lead pencils), diamond, the wonderfully named 'buckyballs' (which are minute spheres of graphite), and graphene (which is a one atom thick layer of graphite). Scientists are very excited about graphene because it's strong, light, almost transparent, and conducts both heat and electricity very well.

The scientific name of the diamond star is BPM 37093. What a mouthful!

Diamond

Diamond is the hardest naturally occurring material and most diamonds are mined in Africa. The largest diamond ever found was the Cullinan, which weighed over 600 grams! It was cut into over 100 smaller diamonds, some of which are part of the Crown Jewels.

The diamond star

Astronomers have found the remains of a massive star, which has been transformed into a huge diamond – a diamond that may be five times the size of the Earth!

Global warming

Fossil fuels (coal, gas and oil) were originally living things, so contain lots of carbon. When we burn them, they release carbon dioxide gas, which collects in the atmosphere and traps extra heat from the sun there. This is known as the Greenhouse Effect, and many scientists are worried that it is leading to climate change.

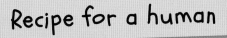

Recipe for a human

Which elements are you made of? And how much of them do you need to make a human?

A 70 kilogram adult is mostly made of:

O	43kg oxygen
C	16kg carbon
H	7kg hydrogen
N	1.8kg nitrogen
Ca	1kg calcium
P	780g phosphorus
K	140g potassium
S	140g sulphur
Na	100g sodium
Cl	95g chlorine
Mg	19g magnesium
Fe	4.2g iron
F	2.6g fluorine
Zn	2.3g zinc
Si	1.0g silicon

N
Nitrogen
Non-Metal

Almost 80% of the air around us is made up of nitrogen. We breathe it in and out, but we don't use it for anything in our bodies. It is vital for plant growth, but is often in short supply in its useable forms, so modern farming relies on adding artificially produced nitrate fertiliser to soil, so that plants can grow well.

Liquid nitrogen has a temperature of −196 degrees Celsius. If you put a banana into liquid nitrogen it will freeze so hard that you can use it to hammer a nail into a plank of wood! It is used (liquid nitrogen, that is, not a frozen banana) as a refrigerant to preserve embryos for in vitro fertilisation.

Laughing gas

Laughing gas is nitrous oxide. It was used as an anaesthetic to relieve pain without knocking the patient out. Although many people found it made them sleepy, it also gave some people the giggles, hence its name. In the 1800s rich people sometimes had laughing gas parties because of the enjoyable effects it caused.

Explosives

Dynamite was invented by Alfred Nobel in 1866 and the money he made from it funds the Nobel Prizes – including, ironically, the Nobel Peace Prize! Nitro-glycerine is a highly explosive liquid. TNT is used in armour piercing shells. Azide is an explosive that saves lives – it's what makes car airbags inflate so quickly. All these explosives contain different compounds of nitrogen.

Atomic number 4

Be
Beryllium
Metal

This is only generated by exploding supernovae (giant exploding stars), so not very common at all. It can be found as crystals of the ore beryllium, up to six metres long!

Atomic number 3

Li

Lithium

Metal

This was the third element created by the Big Bang. It's the lightest metal, and is very reactive – because of this it has to be stored under oil or coated in petroleum jelly as it can burst into flame when it comes into contact with water and oxygen. Lithium carbonate is an important treatment for some mental health problems.

Atomic number 5

B

Boron

Non-Metal

Boron is the lightest metalloid, and its mixture of properties gives it many uses. Without boron, there would be no Silly Putty, Queen Elizabeth I wouldn't have had her white complexion, and we'd be missing one colour of green from fireworks. Boron is always found combined with other elements, and although it has been used for hundreds of years, it wasn't until 1892 that Ezekiel Weintraub managed to isolate it.

Home made Silly Putty

Ask a grown up to help you make your own Silly Putty using this recipe!

I Tablespoon of borax (you can buy this online)

3/8 cup of water

1/4 cup of PVA glue

Food colouring

• Dissolve the borax in 1/8 cup of water.

• Slowly mix the rest of the water into the glue and add a few drops of food colouring.

• Stir the two mixtures together. If it's too sticky, add a little more borax until it's stiff enough.

• Store in a sealed plastic container in the fridge or it will go mouldy!

• Silly Putty flows like a liquid but bounces like a rubber ball.

19

O
Oxygen
Non-Metal

The most common element on Earth, Oxygen makes up 20% of every breath you take. It's needed in order to burn fuel like coal, gas or petrol so they can release the energy they contain. This happens in your body too. The oxygen you breathe in is used in all your cells to release energy from the food you eat.

When Earth first formed, there was no oxygen in the atmosphere. It wasn't until plants evolved and began to produce it by the process of photosynthesis that most of it was made.

Here are some things I bet you didn't know about oxygen.

Sun

Ozone layer

Earth

Ozone: Goody or baddy?

Most oxygen molecules are made of two oxygen atoms, but some are made of three. These are called ozone molecules and they create a thin layer of ozone about 20 kilometres above Earth. This protects us by absorbing over 90% of the harmful UV radiation in sunlight. In recent years the ozone layer has been getting thinner due to man-made pollution. However, the damage seems to be slowing down now that some of the chemicals involved have been banned. So ozone must be a goody then?

Not always. Low-level ozone is definitely a baddy. It can worsen asthma and bronchitis and damage the surface of the lungs. It also damages plant leaves.

Northern Lights

Also known as the Aurora Borealis, these are spectacular bands of light that appear in Northern skies in the right atmospheric conditions. They show up as green or crimson 'curtains' of light when cosmic rays interact with oxygen molecules in the outer atmosphere, and move about as the rays are pulled around by the Earth's magnetic field. The best places to see them are Iceland, Greenland and northern Scandinavia, but you can also see them from the north of Scotland.

Northern Lights, Iceland.

Stevie Wonder

The American singer-songwriter Stevie Wonder has been blind since shortly after birth. It's reported that this is because when he was born prematurely he was given extra oxygen. Unfortunately, high concentrations of oxygen can cause abnormal growth of the blood vessels in the retina at the back of the eye, and in his case it caused him to go blind.

Atomic number 9

F
Fluorine
Non-Metal

Pure fluorine is a pale yellow gas, but it's always found as part of compounds in nature. There are things containing fluorine all over your house, but you wouldn't want to meet it as fluorine gas, which is so reactive that it will make almost anything – even glass – burst into flames.

You'll meet it as fluoride, in your toothpaste, where it helps keep your teeth strong (though too much will turn them brown). Some waterproof materials used to make rain jackets are made using fluorine as well.

Sodium compounds give the sea its salty taste and we use sodium chloride (salt) as our favourite food flavouring. Sodium is needed for our nerves to work. Part of the Roman soldier's wage was money to buy salt and this is where the word 'salary' comes from.

Salinas Grandes, Salt desert, Argentina Andes.

Crystals

Crystals are solids where molecules are arranged in a highly organised 3D pattern. Crystals include sodium chloride – in other words, salt-diamonds and snowflakes. Crystals have flat faces called facets, with sharp edges. Why not grow your own?

Unfortunately, you can't grow diamonds so easily.

Growing salt crystals

You will need:

1/4 cup of salt

1 cup of boiling water

2 teaspoons of vinegar

A piece of sponge (bath not cake!)

Food colouring (optional)

• Get an adult to help you mix the boiling water, salt, vinegar and food colouring (if using) and stir well.

• Put the sponge in a shallow dish.

• Pour enough mixture over the sponge in order to soak it completely and cover the bottom of the dish. Keep the rest for later.

• Leave the dish on a windowsill or somewhere warm and airy. Crystals should start to form within 24 hours.

• As the liquid in the dish evaporates, add more mixture and see how big you can get the crystals to grow.

Atomic number 12

Mg

Magnesium
Metal

Plants need magnesium to be able to photosynthesise (make their own food) and we need it to prevent our bones from becoming brittle. Plants take in magnesium compounds from soil through their roots, but obviously we can't do the same and so we have to eat it. The good news? Chocolate is a good source of magnesium!

Magnesium burns with an intense white light and was once used in photographic flashbulbs. It was also used in the firebombs that were dropped on cities during World War II.

Atomic number 13

Al

Aluminium
Metal

Aluminium is the most common metal on Earth, but when it was first discovered in the 1800s it was more expensive than gold. This was because it was very difficult to purify from the minerals in which it was found. Now that an easy method has been discovered to isolate it, aluminium is used to make everything from soft drink cans to car bodies to racing bikes because it's very light.

It's also a good conductor of heat, which is why it's used in cooking foil, and a good reflector of heat, which is why it's used in spacecraft. It's a very good idea to recycle it, because it takes a lot of energy to make it.

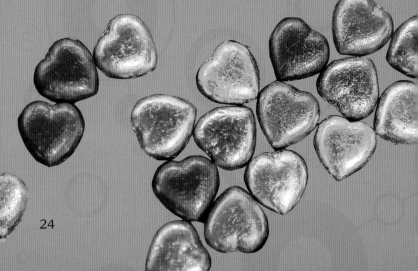

Most soil and rock has lots of silicon in it. Lots of precious and semi-precious stones such as emerald, jade and amethyst also contain silicon. Silicon is used to make everything from bricks and glass to silicon chips and solar cells.

Silicon chips

Silicon chips control everything from your phone, to your computer, to your microwave. They are sometimes called 'integrated circuits' and were a huge step forward from conventional electronic circuits because they could be made much smaller and were much cheaper. This meant that very complex circuits only took up a tiny space. The first silicon integrated circuit was developed in 1959.

Arrowheads

In the Stone Age, knives and arrowheads were made from flint – a compound of silicon and oxygen that could be split to give very sharp edges.

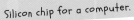
Silicon chip for a computer.

Today's chips can contain millions of times more information than the early versions.

Atomic number 15

P
Phosphorus
Non-Metal

This was the first element to be discovered in modern times and was first isolated from human urine by a German alchemist who was trying to make the Philosopher's Stone. It's highly toxic, but there is lots of it in your body in the form of calcium phosphate, which is the main ingredient of bones and teeth. It's very reactive, which is why it's used to make match heads.

Operation Hamburg after the bombing of Gomorrah.

In World War II, tons of burning phosphorus was dropped on Hamburg by the Allies (the countries who fought against Nazi Germany), destroying most of the city in Operation Gomorrah.

Atomic number 16

S
Sulphur
Non-Metal

Sulphur is a bright yellow non-metal made in volcanic eruptions, both on land and on the seabed. It used to be called Brimstone (which means 'burnstone'). This is why sulphur is also associated with the devil. Sulphur itself doesn't smell, but lots of sulphur compounds do – they give garlic, mustard, cabbage and skunks their smell.

Skunk smell

This can temporarily blind you. It makes your eyes water, and can cause nausea and breathing difficulties in people with asthma. It's very difficult to get rid of the smell. Because of this people drive round dead skunks, not over them!

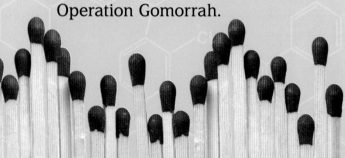

Sulphur medicines

These have been used for hundreds of years. Brimstone and treacle was a popular Victorian laxative, and sulphonamide drugs are still used to treat gut infections.

Gunpowder

Gunpowder is a mixture of sulphur, charcoal and saltpetre (potassium nitrate). When it was first made, it had to be bashed into a powder by people with hammers. Not a great job, as it would often explode. Now, gunpowder is mainly used in fireworks.

Mustard gas

Mustard gas is a deadly poisonous gas that contains sulphur. It's easy to make and use, and damages cells lining the lungs. Mustard gas was used during World War I.

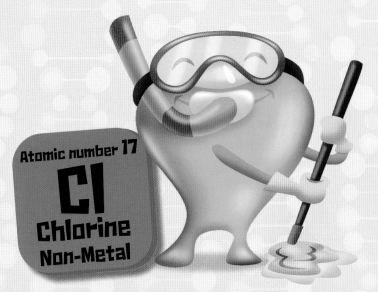

Atomic number 17
Cl
Chlorine
Non-Metal

Chlorine was originally given the much less snappy name of 'dephlogisticated muriatic acid air' when it was described in the 1630s. However, it had been known and used for thousands of years – most commonly in the form of sodium chloride (salt).

Most disinfectants and bleaches are chlorine compounds, and drinking water in many countries is treated with chlorine to kill microbes, helping to wipe out diseases like typhoid and cholera. However, it can also be deadly. Chlorine gas was used as a poison in the trenches of World War I, killing over 5000 soldiers.

Atomic number 19

K
Potassium
Metal

Why K? It's from the medieval Latin word kalium, for ash from which potassium was first isolated.

It has many uses, including being used as a fertiliser and meat preservative. It's vital for nerves to work properly. If you sweat a lot, you can lose so much potassium that you get cramps and muscle weakness. However, you can easily replace the missing potassium by eating a banana, which is why they are the snack of choice for many tennis players.

Atomic number 20

Ca
Calcium
Metal

Calcium is a silvery metal, but most of the things you will come across that contain calcium are white, for example, chalk, bones, teeth or the white cliffs of Dover. Bones and teeth are made of calcium phosphate whereas the cliffs (and chalk) are made from calcium carbonate, and are the skeletons of billions of tiny, long-dead organisms.

The expression 'stealing the limelight' meant taking attention away from another actor by standing in the light.

Lighting in the theatre used to be created by burning calcium oxide in a jet of hydrogen. Because calcium oxide is sometimes called 'lime' this was called 'limelight'.

Atomic number 21

Sc
Scandium
Metal

This is one of the elements that Mendeleev predicted should exist. Ten years after his prediction, it was discovered, but it wasn't until 1937 that someone managed to produce a lump of it, as it only occurs in trace amounts in the Earth's crust. Adding tiny amounts to aluminium makes a very strong alloy, which is used in aircraft.

Atomic number 22

Ti
Titanium
Metal

This is a very strong, but light metal, and won't rust away in seawater like iron. Because of this it is often used to make submarine hulls. It is also used to make replacement hip joints, and the pins and plates that are sometimes used to mend broken bones. It is named after the Titans – a race of giants – in Greek mythology.

Atomic number 24

Cr
Chromium
Metal

Chromium is a silvery white metal, but it's what gives emeralds and rubies their colours. It's used as a corrosion-proof plating on steel and used to give classic cars – especially American ones – their shiny bumpers.

Atomic number 23

V
Vanadium
Metal

Another very strong but light metal, it was used in the steel alloy that was used to manufacture the first mass-produced car, the Model T Ford.

Model T Ford.

29

Atomic number 26

Fe
Iron
Metal

Iron is the most widely used metal. The Iron Age began 3000 years ago when people learned to smelt iron from iron ore, or possibly from meteorites. Blacksmiths were regarded as almost magical because it seemed as if they could turn rock into metal.

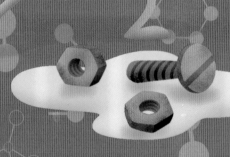

Here are some more amazing facts about iron.

King Arthur

In the legend of King Arthur, he proves he is the rightful king by 'drawing forth the sword from the stone and anvil'. This is usually shown as him freeing a sword stuck through a big stone and a blacksmith's anvil. However, some people think this refers to forging a sword from a stone (meteorite) on an anvil — so maybe King Arthur was a blacksmith!

Rust

Iron is very reactive. One unwelcome result of this is that it will corrode if it is not protected by painting or galvanising it (coating with zinc). This corrosion is called rust, and is a compound called hydrated iron oxide. You can see this process for yourself if you put an iron or steel nail in a dish of water. It should start to rust in a few days.

Blood

In your blood there are millions of tiny red blood cells. They are full of a chemical called haemoglobin, which allows the cells to carry oxygen. Haemoglobin contains iron.

If you don't get enough iron in your diet, your blood can't carry enough oxygen.

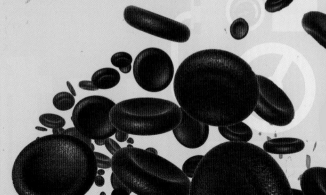

31

Atomic number 25

Mn
Manganese
Metal

Most manganese is found on the seabed in the form of nodules – lumps of manganese minerals that form around a central particle in the same way that a pearl forms round a piece of grit. It is used in glass making to remove iron compounds and as a result creates very clear glass. It was used many thousands of years ago by the earliest artists, as the black colour in cave paintings is manganese oxide.

Atomic number 28

Ni
Nickel
Metal

Nickel is one of the four magnetic elements (the others are iron, cobalt and gadolinium). It's often used in coins, which is why the American five-cent coin is known as a nickel. It's also used to make cheap jewellery, especially earrings, but some people can become allergic to it.

The nodules of manganese are the size of potatoes.

Atomic number 27

Co
Cobalt
Metal

This is named after the German word for goblin – kobald – because the 16th century German miners who discovered it thought it was cursed! Cobalt chloride can be used to make invisible ink. You write a secret message in invisible ink, then write a 'fake' letter on top of it with ordinary ink. When you heat the paper, the invisible message appears, as if by magic…

Cobalt

Atomic number 29

Cu
Copper
Metal

Copper has been used for thousands of years, often made into alloys with other metals. The Bronze Age was named after the alloy of copper and tin, which was used to make weapons, coins and jewellery. Now it is used in electrical wires and printed circuit boards. It is used a lot in building, as it weathers to a green finish known as verdigris. The best known example of this is probably the Statue of Liberty in New York.

Atomic number 31

Ga
Gallium
Metal

This is a metal which melts at under 30 degrees Celsius, so you could hold it in your hand and watch it melt! Chemists who like practical jokes have been known to make teaspoons out of it, which melt when you stir your tea. It is also used in mobile phones and computers. Gallium nitride is the 'blue' in Blu-ray discs.

Atomic number 30

Zn
Zinc
Metal

Zinc is vital for health, and according to research, two billion people don't get enough of it. In areas where there isn't enough zinc in the soil, crops don't grow properly. Maple syrup is a very rich source.

Bring on the pancakes!

Atomic number 32

Ge
Germanium
Metalloid

Metalloid Germanium is named after Germany and is another element which Mendeleev predicted would be found. It was first discovered in silver ore, and can be extracted during production of zinc from ore. It was used as one of the first semi-conductors. It is sold in some countries as a nutritional supplement in its inorganic form, even though it is actually harmful!

Atomic number 33

As
Arsenic
Metalloid

Highly toxic, but was used in a medicine called Salvarsen to treat parasitic blood infections. It has long been used as a poison. For many years, people thought that the French Emperor Napoleon was deliberately poisoned, because traces of arsenic were found in his hair after his death. Now it looks as though he was murdered by his wallpaper! When he was in exile on the island of St Helena, the green wallpaper in his bedroom was made using a dye that contained arsenic. When it got damp, it gave off arsenic-containing gas.

Atomic number 34

Se
Selenium
Non-Metal

Selenium is silvery and shiny, just like lots of metals, but it is a non-metal. Its name comes from the Greek word 'selene' meaning the moon. You are most likely to come across it in the much less exotic surroundings of your bathroom, where it is used in anti-dandruff shampoos.

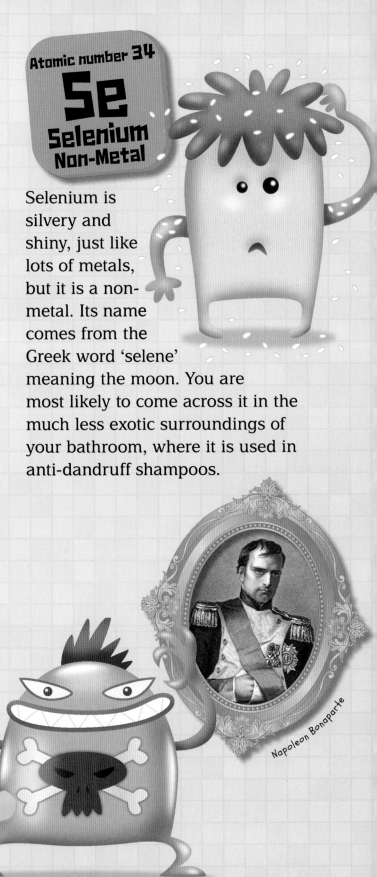

Napoleon Bonaparte

Atomic number 35
Br
Bromine
Non-Metal

Its name means 'stench' in Greek and pure bromine is a liquid at room temperature. It's usually found in the form of bromine salts in seawater and some mineral springs. If you were very rich in ancient times, you might have your clothes dyed Tyrian purple, using a bromine-containing pigment extracted from a type of sea snail. Yuck!

Atomic number 38
Sr
Strontium
Metal

Named after the Scottish village of Strontian, where it was discovered. It has a very harmful radioactive isotope, strontium-90. Huge areas were contaminated with this by the Chernobyl nuclear disaster in Russia in 1986.

Atomic number 39
Y
Yttrium
Metal

Used when making lasers and superconductors, and in cancer treatments. The isotope yttrium-90 can be used to make needles that are more precise than surgical scalpels and can be used in delicate spinal surgery.

Atomic number 37
Rb
Rubidium
Metal

Rubidium is such a reactive metal that if you don't store it under oil, it will burst into flames in air. It is mildly radioactive and can be used to give a purple colour to fireworks.

Atomic number 40
Zr
Zirconium
Metal

If you want to buy a diamond, but can't afford it, this is the next best thing. Zirconium dioxide forms crystals that, to most people, look just like diamonds, even though zirconium itself is a soft grey metal.

Atomic number 41

Nb
Niobium
Metal

This metal can be used to make commemorative coins in lots of different colours by reacting niobium with oxygen. The Native American Full Moon coins produced in Canada in 2011 are each unique because of the way this was done.

Atomic number 42

Mo
Molybdenum
Metal

Confusingly, the name comes from the Greek word for Lead, because its ore used to get confused with lead ore. It was used in armour plating on tanks in World War I.

In the body, molybdenum is found in tooth enamel.

Atomic number 43

Tc
Technetium
Metal

This is one of Mendeleev's 'missing elements' and chemists searched for it for years. After many false alarms, its existence was finally confirmed in 1936. It is a radioactive metal, mostly made inside nuclear reactors. It is used in several types of medical imaging such as the SPECT scan.

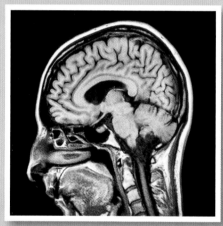

SPECT scan.

Atomic number 44

Ru
Ruthenium
Metal

One of the rarest metals on Earth. It is very resistant to corrosion, so is sometimes used as very thin plating on much cheaper metals. It may soon be used in solar cells and as part of data storage systems on hard discs.

Atomic number 46

Pd
Palladium
Metal

Like rhodium, this silvery-white metal is used in catalytic converters. It is also used to make an alloy of gold – white gold – for use in jewellery.

Atomic number 48

Cd
Cadmium
Metal

You might have rechargeable batteries in your house that contain nickel and cadmium, though they are now being replaced by less toxic ones. Cadmium is hugely toxic to humans and to the environment. On the other hand, without it, Claude Monet couldn't have painted his awesome pictures. One of his favourite colours was cadmium yellow.

Atomic number 45

Rh
Rhodium
Metal

Almost 80% of the rhodium that is produced worldwide is used in catalytic converters, which make the emissions from car engines much less damaging to the environment. It is also a precious metal, and is sometimes used to symbolise great wealth or honour. Paul McCartney was given a rhodium plated disc by the Guinness Book of World Records in 1979 in recognition of the fact that he was the bestselling recording artist and songwriter of all time.

Paul McCartney

Atomic number 47

Ag
Silver
Metal

Silver was first used in Egypt over 5000 years ago. Since its discovery it has been used for a variety of different things, for example mirrors and jewellery. It was used in photographic film (before digital cameras) because silver salts are light-sensitive and change to silver when exposed to light. This made a pattern of light and dark, which could be processed into a black and white photograph. Light-sensitive silver salts are now used in photo reactive glasses – the kind that get darker in sunlight.

Mirrors

Mirrors were originally sheets of polished metal, like bronze or sometimes silver. 'Looking glasses' were first used in the Middle Ages and were made from glass with silver foil behind them. Now the silver is chemically bonded to the glass to make modern mirrors more durable.

Silver nitrate

Previously this was used as an antiseptic, as silver is deadly to many bacteria and viruses. It is now put in some paints to make antibacterial surfaces.

Silver linings in clouds

'Every cloud has a silver lining' just might be true... Silver iodide is dropped from aircraft or fired from rockets into clouds in 'cloud seeding', a method of trying to produce rain.

Indium is used in LCD screens.

Atomic number 49

In

Indium
Metal

Not named after India, but after the Latin word for indigo. It's used in LCD televisions, liquid crystals and solar cells, and it's running out fast. We may only have 20 years supply left. Weirdly – if you bend a piece of indium, it screams! It's the crystals rearranging themselves.

Atomic number 50

Sn

Tin
Metal

This metal screams as well, if you break a bar of it. It's used for coating steel to make tin cans because it doesn't get corroded by acidic food. In Britain, most tin was mined in Cornwall, but the last tin mine closed in 1998. Pewter is an alloy of lead and tin which was widely used for tankards and plates until the 19th century.

Very rare on Earth, but used to make DVD and Blu-ray discs. It's toxic, and someone poisoned with tellurium has breath that smells of garlic (but then, so does someone who has been eating garlic!).

Antimony is toxic and was often used to get rid of inconvenient relatives in the 19th century. Some people think that it was used to poison the composer Mozart in 1791. If you get the dose right though, it can be used as a laxative. In the Middle Ages, antimony pills could be bought as re-useable laxatives: you swallowed one, then waited for it to reappear! Yuck!

Mozart

Iodine compounds can be isolated easily from seawater. It is vital for humans and many other animals. It is needed by the body to make chemicals which help control how food is broken down to release energy. Nowadays it is added to salt, but previously the only way to get enough was by eating sea fish. Before refrigerated transport, this meant that if you lived a long way from the sea, you probably didn't get enough. The iodine is used in the thyroid gland in your neck, to make important chemical messengers. If you don't get enough, this gland grows extra big, leading to a condition called goitre.

Atomic number 55
Cs
Caesium
Metal

This is a spectacularly reactive element that explodes in water, and has to be stored under oil and handled in a non-reactive atmosphere. Large quantities of Cs-137, the radioactive isotope, were released into the atmosphere by the Chernobyl nuclear explosion. It spread on the wind across huge areas of Europe, contaminating soil and affecting livestock. However caesium does have its uses. If you want to know the time really accurately, consult an atomic clock, many of which depend on atomic changes in caesium to work.

Atomic number 56
Ba
Barium
Metal

If you were a witch in the middle ages, what you really needed to impress other witches were some Bologna stones. These were pebbles which, if you left them in the sun for a day, would glow in the dark for days afterwards. These stones contained barite, a compound of barium. Barium is used in 'barium meals' for showing up the stomach and intestines in medical scans.

The Lanthanides

The lanthanides are a group of elements that live in a sort of 'annexe' at the bottom of the periodic table. They share many properties, and are found in the same areas. Many of them were discovered in samples of rock near the village of Ytterby in Sweden.

Atomic number 57 — Lt — Lanthanum — Metal

Lanthanum metal is never found in its pure form. It took a hundred years for someone to work out how to purify it. Among its many uses are making nickel-hydride batteries for hybrid cars and clearing unwanted algae from ponds.

Atomic number 58 — Ce — Cerium — Metal

Cerium looks a bit like iron, but is much softer. Shavings of cerium will burst into flames in contact with air. Cerium is used in catalytic converters.

Atomic number 59 — Pr — Praseodymium — Metal

SLOW

It can be used to colour glass and enamel yellow and is part of a special glass that can slow the speed of light to a few hundred metres per second instead of 299,792,458 metres per second.

Atomic number 60 — Nd — Neodymium — Metal

Neodymium magnets are the strongest magnets you can get. A neodymium magnet can lift 1000 times its own weight.

Atomic number 61 — Pm — Promethium — Metal

This is highly radioactive, so hardly ever occurs naturally, although it can be made in a lab. It can be used to make luminous paint.

Atomic number 62 — Sm — Samarium — Metal

Discovered by the fabulously named Paul Emile Lecoq de Boisbaudran in 1879. Radioactive samarium-153 is used in the treatment of some cancers.

Atomic number 63 — Eu — Europium — Metal

Named after the continent, of course. It doesn't have many uses now, but was vital for making early colour televisions.

Atomic number 64
Gd
Gadolinium
Metal

It's very good at absorbing neutrons, so it is used for shielding in nuclear reactors. It is magnetic, but only up to 19 degrees Celsius.

Atomic number 65
Tb
Terbium
Metal

Pure terbium is soft, silvery-white and very expensive – four times as costly as platinum. Its most interesting use is to make the device called the SoundBug. This is a small speaker that can transform an entire flat surface like metal or wood into a speaker when it is attached to it.

Atomic number 66
Dy
Dysprosium
Metal

Its name means 'hard to get' – and it is. Although it's a metal, it's so soft you can cut it with an ordinary knife. It's needed to make motors for electric cars, among other things, and it may run out as soon as 2015!

Atomic number 67
Ho
Holmium
Metal

Holmium is named after the city of Stockholm. It has the highest magnetic strength of any element and is used in nuclear control rods.

Atomic number 68
Er
Erbium
Metal

Erbium reacts so easily with water or oxygen that it's never found as a pure metal. Your dentist might be using it if you have laser dentistry.

Atomic number 69
Tm
Thulium
Metal

Although it is a metal, Thulium will catch on fire at a lower temperature than paper! It is used in portable x-ray machines.

Atomic number 70
Yb
Ytterbium
Metal

Most is extracted from clay in some areas of China, but it is named after the village of Ytterby in Sweden, where it was first found. Used in pressure gauges that measure explosions and earthquakes.

Atomic number 71
Lu
Lutetium
Metal

This is a very hard, dense metal which, for a long time, was the most costly element to isolate. It is still too rare and expensive to have many uses.

The rocket nozzle of the Apollo Lunar Module contains Hafnium.

Atomic number 74

W

Tungsten
Metal

Also known as Wolfram, which means wolf froth! It is the heaviest element with a biological function – it is used by some bacteria. Until recently it was used for the wire filament in light bulbs.

Atomic number 72

Hf

Hafnium
Metal

Hafnium was one of the last stable elements to be identified, because its chemical properties are so similar to zirconium that scientists found it very difficult to tell them apart. It is used for control rods in pressurised water reactors.

Atomic number 73

Ta

Tantalum
Metal

Because it is corrosion resistant, it is sometimes used to make parts for very expensive watches. It is named after Tantalus, a figure in Greek mythology, who was punished after his death by having food and drink constantly just out of reach.

Atomic number 75

Re

Rhenium
Metal

It was the last stable element to be discovered, in 1925 – not surprising, since the scientists concerned had to process 660 kilograms of molybdenite ore to get one gram of it. Used in superalloys to make jet engine parts.

Atomic number 76

Os
Osmium
Metal

Osmium is the densest element and hardest metal. It is named after the Greek word 'osme' which means smell, so it's really called Smellium! It is used in electron microscopy and is the least abundant stable element in the Earth's crust.

Atomic number 77

Ir
Iridium
Metal

Rare on Earth, but common in meteorites, including the one that some scientists think may have led to the extinction of the dinosaurs. A meteorite around ten kilometres wide crashed to Earth in the Gulf of Mexico near the Yucatan peninsula, leaving a crater about 300 kilometres wide. It left an iridium-rich layer of clay. When the meteorite struck, it sent up a huge dust cloud that blocked so much sunlight that most plants could no longer photosynthesise. The animals – including dinosaurs – which depended on these plants died out.

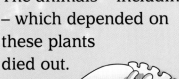

Atomic number 78

Pt
Platinum
Metal

Platinum is a precious metal – even more precious than gold, and it has been used to make jewellery for at least 2000 years. Interestingly, although there were silver and gold rushes, there was never a platinum rush, even though you can find it in some river sands, like gold. The International Prototype Kilogram (which defines exactly what a kilogram is) is a cylinder of platinum-iridium alloy made in 1879. A record that sells more than one million copies has 'gone platinum'. Platinum is used in catalytic converters, electrodes, and in cancer treatments.

Atomic number 79

Au
Gold
Metal

The symbol comes from the Latin word for gold – aurum. Most other metals are silver in colour, but gold is gold coloured because its electrons move so fast.

Gold is one of the rarest elements on Earth. Most of it exists in seawater, but it is too dispersed to be collected. It is popular for jewellery because it stays bright and untarnished indefinitely. The biggest nugget of gold ever found was the Welcome Stranger, mined in Victoria, Australia in 1858, and weighing in at an impressive 72.04 kilograms. It was melted down in London in 1859.

Here are some more nuggets of information about gold.

The California Gold Rush

This took place between 1848 and 1855, and brought 300,000 people to California. San Francisco was a village of 200 people when it started and by 1852, it was a city of 36,000. However, this wasn't the only gold rush. They also took place in Alaska, Australia and South Africa.

Preparing the fields for the gold extraction.

Panning for gold

This is a very ancient way of extracting gold from river gravel. Water is swirled over the gravel in a special shallow pan. The lighter bits are washed out, but because gold is so heavy, it stays at the bottom of the pan. You can even pan for gold in parts of the UK!

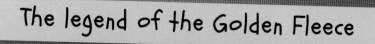

The legend of the Golden Fleece

One of the Greek myths is about how the hero Jason stole the Golden Fleece. Some people think this is based on fact, as another way to extract gold from rivers is to suspend a sheep fleece in the water. The gold fragments get caught in the wool, and if there are enough, the fleece would look golden.

What is a carat?

The purity of gold is measured in carats. Twenty-four carat gold is pure gold. Eighteen carat gold has 18/24 parts gold, 9 carat is 9/24 parts gold, and so on.

Not the vegetable!

47

The old name for mercury was 'quicksilver' and its symbol comes from the Latin word 'hydragyrum', which means liquid silver. It is the only metal that is a liquid at room temperature, (the only other element that is liquid at room temperature is bromine) and it's so dense that even lead will float on it.

Thermometers used to contain mercury, but many now contain alcohol instead, as mercury is quite toxic. It is used in the silvery amalgam used to fill teeth – but it isn't toxic in this amalgam. It was used in lots of medicines before people realised how harmful it was, and is still used in many types of mascara. In Moorish Spain, some of the palace gardens had mercury reflecting-pools in them for visitors to look into (and dip their fingers into, which wasn't such a great idea).

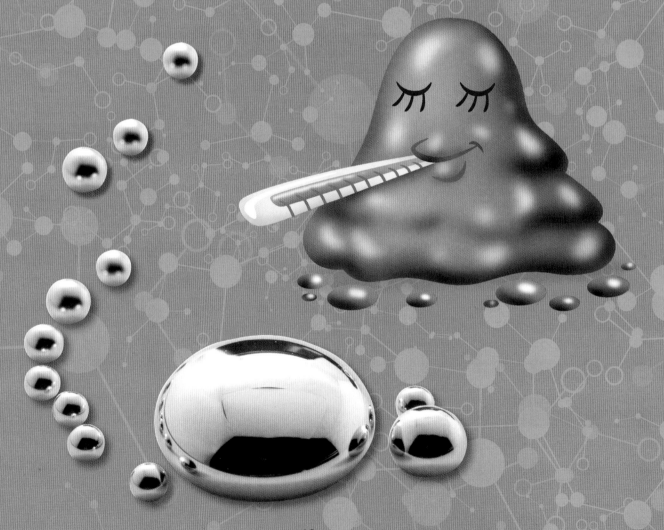

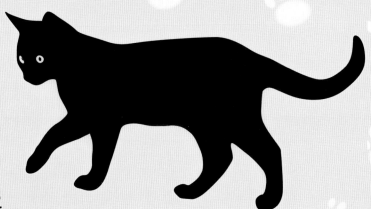

Minamata disease

Methylmercury was released in industrial waste water into the sea near the Japanese city of Minamata between 1932 and 1968. It contaminated fish and shellfish, which were eaten by the local people, giving them mercury poisoning. Animals were also affected. In cats, it was known as 'dancing cat fever' because of the way in which their movement was affected. In humans it caused numbness, damage to hearing and speech and, in some cases, paralysis, insanity, coma and death. Over 2200 victims suffered from Minamata disease.

Mad as a hatter

If you've read *Alice in Wonderland*, you'll have come across the Mad Hatter. Lewis Carroll didn't just dream this up at random though. In Victorian times Mad Hatter Disease was well known and was caused by the use of mercury compounds in the production of felt for fur hats.

Atomic number 81

Tl
Thallium
Metal

Known as 'the poisoner's poison' because it was often used in murders. Thallium sulphate was easy to buy as it used to be sold as rat poison. It was soluble, tasteless, odourless and hard to detect in the body.

Arrghh!

'Aunt Thally' Grills

One of Australia's most famous murder cases featured thallium poisoning. In 1953, 63-year-old Caroline Grills was convicted of killing four members of her family and trying to kill another two by putting thallium sulphate in their tea. In prison in Sydney, she was nicknamed 'Aunt Thally'. This was just one of a spate of thallium murders in Australia at that time.

Agatha Christie

Agatha Christie used thallium to kill the victims in her book *The Pale Horse*. In doing so, she also saved some real lives, as at least two readers recognised the symptoms of thallium poisoning once they had read it!

Agatha Christie

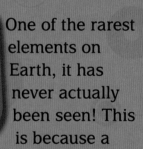

Atomic number 83

Bi
Bismuth
Metal

A silvery-pink metal, mostly obtained as a by-product of copper and tin production. Probably best known as an ingredient of some over-the-counter treatments for stomach problems.

Bismuth is also used as a pigment in nail varnish and eye shadow.

Atomic number 85

At
Astatine
Metal

One of the rarest elements on Earth, it has never actually been seen! This is because a piece big enough to be seen would vaporise in the heat generated by its radioactivity. Probably less than one gram exists on Earth at any time.

The most unstable of the natural elements, it's almost impossible to investigate, so not a lot is known about it, and it doesn't have any commercial uses.

51

Lead is the heaviest metal and gets its symbol from the Latin word 'plumbum'. Until fairly recently most water pipes were made of lead – this is why we call people who fix water pipes plumbers.

It was a good idea in one respect as lead is easy to mould and bend, so you can make pipes that go round corners. However it was also a very bad idea since lead is toxic. Nowadays copper is used to make pipes instead. Lead has had various uses for thousands of years because it is easy to obtain and to work.

Let me lead you through some facts about lead...

Queen Elizabeth I

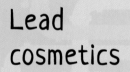

Lead cosmetics

It's amazing what people will put on their faces. In the past, people used white lead in powders and pastes to give them a fashionably pale complexion, even though they knew it could lead to bad skin, baldness and even death!

Lead pigments

These were used in paints, but this has now been discontinued due to the toxicity of lead. It was a particularly bad move to paint baby cots with lead paint, as babies sometimes chew at the cot bars when they are teething.

Thomas Midgely

Thomas Midgely was an American engineer who, in 1921, discovered that adding a little tetraethyl lead to petrol made car engines work much better. Petrol manufacturers took a long time to realise that the signs of poisoning that many of their workers began to show was connected to this, but eventually scientists realised that leaded petrol was a major pollutant, affecting humans and the environment. Now, most petrol is lead-free.

Thomas Midgely may hold the unenviable record of doing more harm to the environment than any other human being, as he also developed chemicals known as CFCs, which until recently were widely used in refrigeration, aerosols and polystyrene packaging. When released into the atmosphere, these chemicals head straight for the ozone layer and hang around for thousands of years, constantly damaging it.

The Franklin Expedition

This was an Arctic exploration voyage that ended in disaster. The expedition set out from England in 1845, but never returned. Searches eventually found the remains of the expedition, including several graves. Studies of the bodies suggested that some people were poisoned by the lead which was, at the time, used to solder cans of food, but it now looks as though lots of people at that time had similar levels of lead in their bodies without suffering harm.

Pierre Curie

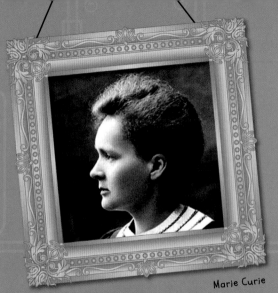

Marie Curie

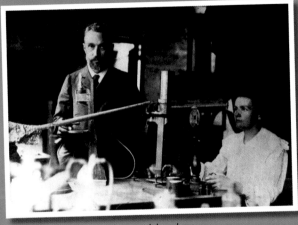

Atomic number 84

Po
Polonium
Metalloid

The most highly political element in the periodic table, deadly poisonous polonium, was discovered by the Curies in 1898. They named it after their native country of Poland, in a move to publicise Poland's lack of independence at the time. The first death from polonium poisoning may have been the Curies' daughter Irene Joliot-Curie, who died from leukaemia some years after a capsule of polonium exploded on the bench where she was working.

Marie and Pierre Curie working in a laboratory.

Marie and Pierre Curie

Marie and Pierre Curie spent years studying uranium ore, and found that it contained other elements too – radium and polonium. In 1903 they were awarded the Nobel Prize for Physics, along with Henri Becquerel. Marie was the first woman ever to win one. In 1911, she was awarded another Nobel Prize – this time for Chemistry – for her work on radium (Pierre had died in 1906). She developed mobile x-ray units and drove ambulances containing them during World War I. She died of aplastic anaemia in 1934, probably as a result of her exposure to radiation. Even now, Marie Curie's notebooks are so radioactive that they have to be kept in lead lined boxes and handled by people wearing protective clothing.

Assassinations

Polonium has been implicated in political assassinations, most famously that of Russian dissident Alexander Litvinenko in 2006. He fell ill while living in London and died a painful and lingering death in hospital. When his death was investigated traces of polonium were found in his body, and in places in London where he had been just before falling ill.

Atomic number 88

Ra
Radium
Metal

The Curies discovered radium in 1898. It is radioactive and glows in the dark. It became very popular in the early part of the 20th century, before people realised the dangers. It was used in luminous paint, particularly on watch dials. It was painted on by the so-called 'Radium Girls', who often licked their brushes to give them a nice, fine point. Not surprisingly, the girls often became ill. More bizarrely, it was added to toothpaste, hair creams and 'tonics'. Radium was also an important treatment for cancers in the early 20th century.

Atomic number 89

Ac
Actinium
Metal

It is extracted from uranium ore, but this is quite a job, since there is only about 0.2 milligrams of actinium in one tonne of ore! Because it is so scarce, not to mention highly radioactive, it has no commercial uses.

Atomic number 91

Pa
Protactinium
Metal

Very rare, very toxic, and almost entirely useless. It can be extracted – with great difficulty – from uranium ore, but 66 tons of uranium would only give you about 125 grams of protactinium!

Atomic number 90

Th
Thorium
Metal

Named after Thor, the Norse god of thunder. Some countries are researching whether this radioactive element could be used in nuclear reactors instead of uranium.

The Manhattan Project

This was the research project that developed the first atomic bombs during World War II. It involved the USA, the UK and Canada, and work was carried out at more than 30 sites in those three countries. It began in 1939, and led to the production of two types of atomic bomb: one containing uranium and the other plutonium. The project also had to monitor German research into nuclear energy, which involved agents working behind enemy lines.

The first ever nuclear explosion was the Trinity Test, carried out in New Mexico. After the test, the scientific director of the project, J Robert Oppenheimer, famously said, "Now I am become death, the destroyer of worlds" (a quote from Hindu scripture). Near the end of the war, two nuclear bombs were dropped on Japan, the only nuclear weapons ever to have been used. The Manhattan Project continued until 1947.

Atomic bomb explosion.

Atomic number 92

U

Uranium
Metal

The best known of the radioactive elements, it is used in nuclear reactors to supply electricity in many countries. Amazingly, ancient natural nuclear reactor sites have been found in Gabon, West Africa. Known as the Oklo Fossil Reactors, they were active 1.7 billion years ago!

Before it was realised it was radioactive, it was used in glazes for tiles and pottery. Its radioactivity was discovered when Henri Becquerel put a sample of uranium salts into a drawer on top of a photographic plate, and found when he looked at it later that the plate had been fogged by the radioactivity of the uranium.

Nuclear Power plant.

Atomic bombs

Uranium has much more sinister uses in atomic bombs. The first atomic bomb, known as 'Little Boy', was dropped on the Japanese city of Hiroshima on August 6th 1945. The blast killed over 100,000 people. Those who died in the first few days after the bombing were mostly killed by burn or falling debris, but during the next few months, many more died of radiation sickness.

Fictional Elements

Science fiction is very keen on making up new elements. You've already met Kryptonite — here are some more.

Dilithium

The crystals that regulate the Star Ship Enterprise's warp engines in *Star Trek*.

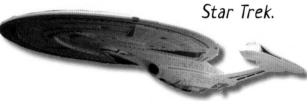

Mithril

A light, strong, silvery metal used by elves to make the mail shirt worn by Bilbo and Frodo Baggins in *The Hobbit* and *The Lord of the Rings*.

Octiron

A dense, black metal found in the crust of Terry Pratchett's *Discworld*.

Unobtainium

The fantastically rare metal being mined on the planet Pandora in the film *Avatar*.

Carbonite

Han Solo is frozen into a block of carbonite at the end of the *Star Wars* film *The Empire Strikes Back*.

And finally... Elements which don't exist but really should.

Yummium
Chemical symbol: Mmm
The tastiest element of them all.

Amazonium
An element only available by mail order.

Gymnasium
Often added to muscle building supplements.

The Quick Particle Guide

Subatomic particles are protons, neutrons and electrons. Together these make up...

Atoms. An atom is the basic unit of an element. It can't be broken down any further by a chemical reaction. Atoms join together to make...

Molecules. Molecules are two or more atoms joined by chemical bonds. For example, an oxygen molecule is O_2 — two atoms of oxygen stuck together. Water is H_2O — two atoms of hydrogen combined with one atom of oxygen. It is a...

Compound. Compounds are substances made of molecules of two or more elements.

Above is a quick guide to the particles we've seen.

The Complete Periodic Table

Find Out More

Read

Itch (Doubleday Childrens, 2012)

A fictional adventure about Itch – an element hunter who wants to collect all of the elements in the periodic table!

Mendeleev on the Periodic Law: Selected Writings, 1869-1905 (Dover Publications, 2012)

A collection of Mendeleev's most important writings on the periodic law.

What Makes You YOU? by Gill Arbuthnott (A & C Black, 2013)

A fantastic guide to DNA, genes and everything that makes you YOU!

Visit

The Royal Scottish Museum of Scotland in Edinburgh to see the 'Restless Earth' gallery, full of fantastic specimens of rocks, meteorites and precious stones.

https://www.nms.ac.uk

The Vault in the Science Museum in London to see precious stones and meteorites.

http://www.sciencemuseum.org.uk

The Jewel Room at The Tower of London to see the fabulous precious stones set into the Crown Jewels, including part of the Cullinan diamond.

http://www.hrp.org.uk/TowerOfLondon/

Log on to

http://www.bbc.co.uk/learningzone/clips/groups-and-periods-in-the-periodic-table/10623.html

A short but informative video about the structure of the periodic table.

http://www.chem4kids.com/extras/quiz_elemintro/index.html

A great interactive quiz that will test your knowledge of the elements!

http://www.bbc.co.uk/radio4/science/puzzle4.shtml

Try out this head scratcher of a puzzle!

Glossary

Abundant Exists in a very large quantity.

Alchemist Someone who studied alchemy, which was what existed before proper, scientific chemistry. Alchemy was a combination of chemistry and magic.

Alloy A metal melted together with another element, which often makes it stronger. Bronze is an alloy of copper and tin.

Amalgam An alloy of mercury and other metals used in dental fillings.

Anaesthetic A substance that stops you feeling pain.

Annexe An extension to the main part of, in this case, the periodic table. (It's where the Lanthanides are shown).

Atom The smallest unit of an element. It is tiny in size and is made up of a positively charged nucleus surrounded by negatively charged electrons.

Atomic number The number of protons in an element.

Commercial use Use of something in order to make money. For instance, one commercial use of aluminium is to make soft drink cans.

Compound Atoms of two or more elements joined together to make molecules.

Conductor A material that carries (conducts) electricity.

Corrosion The gradual destruction of metal, caused by a chemical reaction with its environment.

Electron Particle outside the nucleus of an atom which has negative charge.

Fossil fuel Any fuel that is formed by natural processes (from plant or animal remains) – coal, gas and oil.

Galvanising Coating a metal with zinc in order to protect it from corrosion.

Group Column in the periodic table.

Haemoglobin A chemical in red blood cells that allows them to carry oxygen.

In vitro fertilisation Fertilisation outside the body. Eggs and sperm are mixed in a glass dish.

Isolated Alone – not near to anything else.

Isotopes Forms of the same element with different numbers of neutrons in the nucleus. For example, strontium has 50 neutrons, but radioactive strontium-90 has 52.

Large Hadron Collider A huge particle accelerator in Switzerland. It is used to smash particles – beams of protons, for instance – into each other at great speed to test theories about physics and try to find evidence for the existence of fundamental particles such as the Higgs Boson.

Laxative A medicine used to make it easier to empty your bowels (in other words, something that makes you poo).

Metalloid An element with properties of both a metal and a non-metal.

Mixture Different elements or compounds that are physically close together but not chemically joined.

Neutron Particle in the nucleus of an atom which has no charge.

Noble Gases A group of elements that are extremely unreactive.

Ore Mineral from which metal is extracted.

Period Row in the periodic table.

Philosopher's Stone One of the things that Alchemists tried to make (unsuccessfully). It was meant to give the maker eternal life and allow them to turn metals like lead into gold.

Photosynthesis The process by which plants use energy from sunlight to convert water and carbon dioxide into sugars.

Pigment A substance used to give something colour.

Proton Particle in the nucleus of an atom which has positive charge.

Salary A wage that is paid monthly. From the Latin word for salt – sal – as Roman soldiers got part of their pay to buy salt.

Smelt Melt ore in order to produce metal.

Solder Join pieces of metal together.

Subatomic Part of an atom.

Supernovae Huge, very bright exploding stars.

Theoretical Believed to be possible but so far lacking evidence to support that belief.

Toxic Poisonous.

Transatlantic Across the Atlantic Ocean – for example, from the UK to America.

Index